bite Stone

oel

Jonah

Amos

I & II Kings written

Nahum

Zephaniah

Daniel

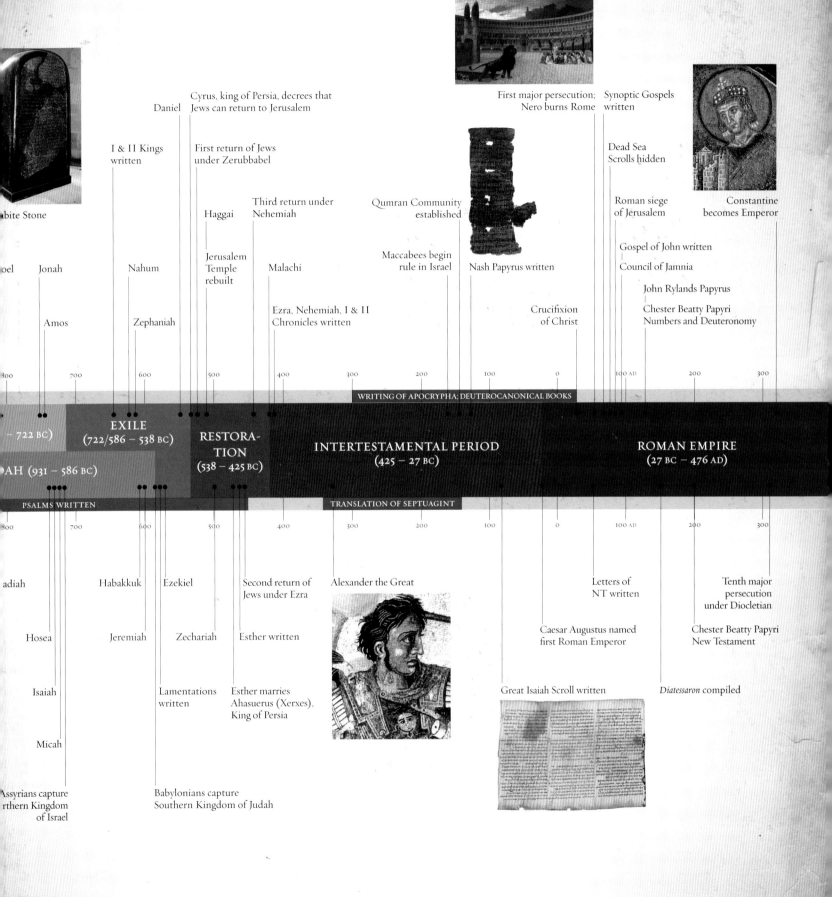

Cyrus, king of Persia, decrees that Jews can return to Jerusalem

First return of Jews under Zerubbabel

Haggai

Jerusalem Temple rebuilt

Third return under Nehemiah

Malachi

Ezra, Nehemiah, I & II Chronicles written

Qumran Community established

Maccabees begin rule in Israel

Nash Papyrus written

First major persecution; Nero burns Rome

Crucifixion of Christ

Synoptic Gospels written

Dead Sea Scrolls hidden

Roman siege of Jerusalem

Gospel of John written

Council of Jamnia

John Rylands Papyrus

Chester Beatty Papyri Numbers and Deuteronomy

Constantine becomes Emperor

800 · 700 · 600 · 500 · 400 · 300 · 200 · 100 · 0 · 100 AD · 200 · 300

WRITING OF APOCRYPHA; DEUTEROCANONICAL BOOKS

– 722 BC)

AH (931 – 586 BC)

EXILE (722/586 – 538 BC)

RESTORATION (538 – 425 BC)

INTERTESTAMENTAL PERIOD (425 – 27 BC)

ROMAN EMPIRE (27 BC – 476 AD)

PSALMS WRITTEN

TRANSLATION OF SEPTUAGINT

800 · 700 · 600 · 500 · 400 · 300 · 200 · 100 · 0 · 100 AD · 200 · 300

adiah

Hosea

Isaiah

Micah

Assyrians capture rthern Kingdom of Israel

Habakkuk

Jeremiah

Ezekiel

Lamentations written

Babylonians capture Southern Kingdom of Judah

Zechariah

Second return of Jews under Ezra

Esther written

Esther marries Ahasuerus (Xerxes), King of Persia

Alexander the Great

Letters of NT written

Caesar Augustus named first Roman Emperor

Great Isaiah Scroll written

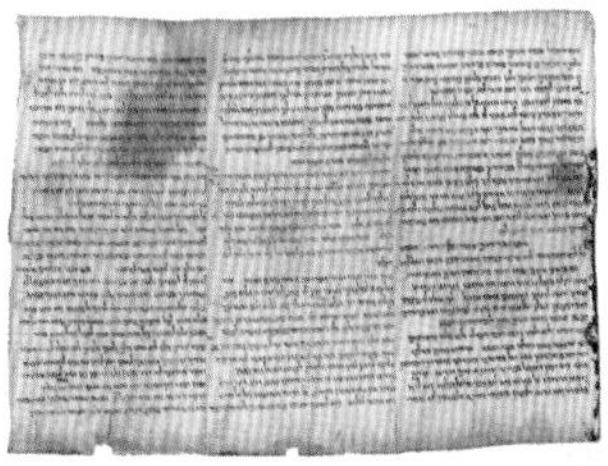

Tenth major persecution under Diocletian

Chester Beatty Papyri New Testament

Diatessaron compiled

THE STORY OF
THE BIBLE

The fascinating history of its writing, translation & effect on civilization.

LARRY STONE

THOMAS NELSON
Since 1798

NASHVILLE DALLAS MEXICO CITY RIO DE JANEIRO

To Clara, Hadassah, Nehemiah, Benaiah, Duncan, Iliyah, Tristan, Noah, and their children,

with the prayer that, in the words of the prefix of the Geneva Bible, the Bible might be the light to their paths, their comfort in affliction, the glass wherein they behold God's face, and the food and nourishment of their souls.

For more stories, up-to-date news, and fascinating links, be sure to visit www.storyofbible.com.

Published in Nashville, Tennessee, by Thomas Nelson. Thomas Nelson is a registered trademark of Thomas Nelson, Inc.

Book and cover design by Don Bailey

Thomas Nelson, Inc., titles may be purchased in bulk for educational, business, fund-raising, or sales promotional use.
For information, please e-mail SpecialMarkets@ThomasNelson.com.

Library of Congress Control Number: 2010922205

ISBN-13: 9781595551191

Printed in Malaysia

10 11 12 13 14 TWP 6 5 4 3 2

CONTENTS

Acknowledgments and Picture Credits 4

Foreword by Raví Zacharias 5

Introduction 7

CHAPTER 1: Beginnings 8

CHAPTER 2: The People of the Book 16

CHAPTER 3: Foundation of a New Faith 28

CHAPTER 4: The Early Years of the Church 36

CHAPTER 5: The Middle Ages 46

CHAPTER 6: The Remarkable Century from Gutenberg to Luther 58

CHAPTER 7: The Bible in English 68

CHAPTER 8: The Old Book in the New World 80

CHAPTER 9: "To the End of the Earth" 90

Acknowledgments

I would like to give special thanks to Sam Moore, a mentor, for giving me opportunities and for his enthusiasm for publishing the Bible; to Rod Gragg, for his encouragement and example; to Dr. Liana Lupus, Curator of the Scripture Collection, for opening the treasures of the American Bible Society Library to me; to Dr. Roy B. Zuck and Dr. Herbert L. Samworth, for their editorial expertise and contributions; to Joel Miller, for his belief in this book; and to Don Bailey, for his superior graphic design skills and being a great person with whom to work.

Picture Credits

Page 9: St. John the Evangelist; AD 1133; Illuminator is unknown; tempura colors, gold leaf, gold paint, and ink on parchment bound between pasteboard covered with olive green calf; size is 22.1 x 18.1 cm (8-11/16" x 7-1/8"); number 83.MB.68.106v; courtesy of The J. Paul Getty Museum, Los Angeles. Page 10: Reproduction of ms. Amiatino 1, cc. 5r courtesy of Biblioteca Medicea Laurenziana di Firenze and reprinted with the permission of the Ministry for Cultural Heritage. Further reproduction by any means is prohibited. Page 11: Ann Ronan Picture Library / HIP / Art Resource, NY. Page 13: www.HolyLandPhotos.org, used by permission of Carl Rasmussen. Page 14: Photo of Mesha Stele courtesy of Wally Gobetz. Page 15: © Richard T. Nowitz/Corbis. Page 17: Photo of Qumran, Israel, aerial view of the caves and settlement from the South, copyright Sonia Halliday Photographs. Page 18: The Granger Collection, New York. Page 19: Image copyright © The Metropolitan Museum of Art / Art Resource, NY. Page 20: Image on folio 6v of eleventh century Octateuch, Vat. gr. 747, © 2010 Biblioteca Apostolica Vaticana. Reproduced by permission of Biblioteca Vaticana, with all rights reserved. Page 22: Werner Forman / Art Resource, NY. Page 23: The Art Archive / Alfredo Dagli Orti. Page 24: © John C. Trever, PhD, digital image James E. Trever. Page 25: © John C. Trever, PhD, digital image James E. Trever. Page 26: Erich Lessing / Art Resource, NY. Page 27: From the collections of the Omaha Public Library (ster_w_00700: Pentateuch Scroll and Priest of the Levites. Nablus, Palestine). Page 29: Quatre évangélistes, folio 19v-20, ms. LATIN 11959, Manuscrits occidentaux, Bibliotèque nationale de France. Page 30: Codex Beneventanus, BL Add. MS 5463, folio 3r, © 2010 The British Library Board. All Rights Reserved. Page 32: Codex Alexandrinus, BL Royal MS 1 D VIII, folio 107v, © 2010 The British Library Board. All Rights Reserved. Page 33: Reproduced by courtesy of the University Librarian and Director, The John Rylands University Library, The University of Manchester. Page 34: Photograph by Matson Photo Service and reproduced courtesy of the Library of Congress. Page 35: http://en.wikipedia.org/wiki/File:Tischendorf_-_stehend.jpg#file. Page 37: St. Jerome, folio 3v entier, ms. LATIN 1, Manuscrits occidentaux, Bibliotèque nationale de France. Page 38: Icon of Ignatius is copyright Holy Transfiguration Monastery, Brookline, Massachusetts, and used with permission. Page 39 (left): The Granger Collection, New York. Page 39 (right): © Francis G. Mayer/Corbis. Page 40: http://en.wikipedia.org/wiki/File:Byzantinischer_Mosaizist_um_1000_002.jpg. Page 41: The Art Archive / Roger Cabal Collection / Gianni Dagli Orti. Page 42: The Art Archive / San Giorgio Schiavoni Naples. Page 44: http://en.wikipedia.org/wiki/File:Eusebius_of_Caesarea.jpg. Page 45: Nag Hammadi Codex II © Institute for Antiquity and Christianity, Claremont, California, and used by permission. Page 47: arbre de Jessé en forme de L, folio 7v, ms. LATIN 16746, Manuscrits occidentaux, Bibliotèque nationale de France. Page 48: folio 295v, ms. LATIN 36, Manuscrits occidentaux, Bibliotèque nationale de France. Page 49: Erich Lessing / Art Resource, NY. Page 50: http://www.kb.se/bilder/Codex/Textill/stetoskopiskbild,m,1.jpg and courtesy of the National Library of Sweden. Page 51 (left): Photo of the Salisbury Cathedral © Dr. John Crook. Page 51 (right): Photo of Chartres Cathedral, aerial view from the South East, copyright Sonia Halliday Photographs. Page 53: The Morgan Picture Bible, (probably Paris), c. 1250, MS. M.638, fol. 23v, reproduced by permission of The Pierpont Morgan Library / Art Resource, NY. Page 55: The Book of Kells, TCD MS 58, folio 104r, reproduced by permission of The Board of Trinity College Dublin. Page 57: The Aleppo Codex, Ms. Ben-Zvi 1, Psalm 119:122-170, courtesy of the Ben-Zvi Institute, Jerusalem. Page 59: The Art Archive / Private Collection / Marc Charmet. Page 60 (left): The Granger Collection, New York. Page 60 (right): The Granger Collection, New York. Page 61 (left): Gutenberg Bible, paper, BL c.9.d.3, Vol. 1, folio 114v, © 2010 The British Library Board. All Rights Reserved. Page 61 (right): Gutenberg Bible, vellum, BL G.12226, Vol. 1, folio 114v, © 2010 The British Library Board. All Rights Reserved. Page 62: The Art Archive / Bibliothèque Universitaire Geneva / Gianni Dagli Orti. Page 63: The Granger Collection, New York; after a painting by Anton von Werner. Page 64 (left): © Alinari Archives/Corbis. Page 64 (right): Photo © by Suzanne Hein-Hoffmann and used by permission. Page 65: http://www-personal.ksu.edu/~lyman/english233/images/Council_of_Trent.jpg. Page 67 (top, left): http://en.wikipedia.org/wiki/File:Holbein-erasmus.jpg. Page 67 (bottom, right): Title page of Complutensian Polyglot courtesy of the American Bible Society library and used by permission. Photograph by Bruce Curtis and © by Lawrence M. Stone. Page 69: Stringer / Hulton Archive / Getty Images; after a painting by Sir George Harvey. Page 70: Painting of William Tyndale courtesy of Hertford College, University of Oxford, and used by permission. Page 71: "William Tyndale Printing His Translation of the Bible into English" by Violet Oakley, photograph by Brian Hunt and courtesy of Pennsylvania Capitol Preservation Committee. Page 72: Title page of Tyndale Bible at Württembergische Landesbibliothek Stuttgart and courtesy of Eberhard Zwink. Page 73: from *Foxe's Book of Martyrs*. Page 74: Detail from "The Family of Henry VIII," artist unknown, The Royal Collection © 2010, Her Majesty Queen Elizabeth II. Page 75: The Great Bible courtesy of the American Bible Society library and used by permission. Photograph by Bruce Curtis and © by Lawrence M. Stone. Page 76: "James I," Paul van Somer, The Royal Collection © 2010, Her Majesty Queen Elizabeth II. Page 77: Photo of Hampton Court Palace courtesy of Marshall Manson. Page 78: http://en.wikipedia.org/wiki/File:Gunpow1.jpg. Page 81: http://en.wikipedia.org/wiki/File:Embarkation_of_the_Pilgrims.jpg. Page 82 (left): color engraving by John Chester Buttre after a drawing by Johannes Adam Simon Oertel, The Granger Collection, New York. Page 82 (right): Title page of Algonquin Bible courtesy of William L. Clements Library, University of Michigan. Page 83: Christopher Saur Bible from the collection of Turpin Library, Dallas Theological Seminary and used by permission. Page 84: The Granger Collection, New York. Page 85: Stringer / AFP / Getty Images. Page 86: *Chicago Tribune* front page courtesy of Footnote.com. Page 87 (left): National Council of Churches photo and used by permission. Page 87 (right): Photo courtesy of Moody Bible Institute of Chicago, Crowell Library Archives. Page 88 (top, left): Photo courtesy of Tyndale House Publishers. Page 88 (bottom, right): Photo courtesy of Thomas Nelson Publishers. Page 91 (clockwise from top left): Lansdale, Pennsylvania – Photo by Holly Stone and used by permission; China – © Michael Reyolds/epa/Corbis; St. John – © Francis G. Mayer/Corbis; St. John – © Francis G. Mayer/Corbis; Tanzania – James Burke / Time & Life Pictures / Getty Images; Middle East – Photo provided courtesy of Biblica and used by permission; Eastern Europe – Photo provided courtesy of Biblica and used by permission; Afghanistan – © David Bathgate/Corbis; San Francisco – Michael Zagaris / Getty Images; Ethiopia – Photo by Marina Poblacion and used by permission; Jerusalem – © Robert Wallis/Corbis; Chicago: Photographs and Prints Division, Schomburg Center for Research in Black Culture, The New York Public Library, Astor, Lenox and Tilden Foundations; Bushnell, Illinois – © Andrew Lichtenstein/Corbis; Ghana – Photo provided courtesy of Biblica and used by permission; Thailand – Photo by Kloie Picot and used by permission; Los Angeles – Mark Ralston / AFP / Getty Images; San Francisco – Michael Zagaris / Getty Images; Macks Creek, Missouri – Photo by Stan D. Sherwood and used by permission. Page 92: 1799 edition of Welsh Bible, BSS.204.D99.1, is in the collection of the British and Foreign Bible Society, Cambridge University Library in England and has been reproduced by kind permission of the Syndics of Cambridge University Library. Page 93: Photo provided courtesy of Biblica and used by permission. Page 94: © Michael Reynolds/epa/Corbis. Page 95: Photo courtesy of the Africa Evangelical Fellowship and used by permission. Page 96: Photo by David J. Ringer and used by permission of Wycliffe Bible Translators.

FOREWORD

As human beings we live with deep hungers that gnaw at our hearts with a desperate constancy: the hunger for truth as lies proliferate; the hunger for love as we see hate wielding its power; the hunger for justice as we see injustice mocking the law; the hunger for forgiveness when we ourselves fail and stumble.

For over three decades I have traveled the globe, speaking in universities and various settings. In many of these venues I have often encountered the much-heralded belief of postmodernism—that truth is unknowable and skepticism on ultimate matters is the only reasonable position, thus freeing us to disregard history and to find our own way forward. But this surrender to skepticism is not the path to freedom; it is the benchmark of our culture's greatest crisis because it restricts meaningful dialogue on questions of the soul and does not address our deepest hungers. This position is also self-defeating unless its claims are true and made with words that have meaning. Indeed, in reality our methods call our bluff when we are confronted with the undeniable relationship between truth and living. In such an atmosphere is it any wonder that a Canadian survey among its young people revealed that the majority stated that their greatest longing in life was to find someone they could believe in? Whether in the East or West, in my travels I hear much the same.

How, then, do we arrive at the truth? For many, the starting point is God, and who He has revealed Himself to be in the Bible. Here we find that God is the eternally existent One, the Absolute, from whom we draw all definitions for life's purpose and destiny. Here we find addressed our hunger for truth, love, justice, and forgiveness.

No book in history has been so studied, so used, and so abused as the Holy Bible. Millions across history have staked their lives on it. Destiny-defining trust has been placed in it. Graveside hope has been based on it. The charters of nations have been built on it. Others with equal intensity have sought to expel it. Extraordinary good has been spread because of it. Wrongheaded zeal has caused untold evil in the name of it.

But above all, its message stands or falls on its authenticity. Is there truth for all of us within its pages, or is it only for those with superstitious and unsuspecting minds? Is the Bible mere fantasy, or is it fantastically true? Is this indeed the Word from God to us, or is it the fraudulent work of a few who claimed divine superintendence?

Larry Stone's *The Story of the Bible* offers a captivating and colorful account of the history of the Bible from parchment to print, and from its English translation to over 2,400 languages. With his selection of pictures and fascinating stories, Larry has done a wonderful job of making scholarly material engaging and accessible to many more readers. Along the way, he shows how the biblical documents have withstood the most scrutinizing analysis ever imposed on any manuscript and have emerged with compelling authenticity and authority. No other ancient literature demonstrates such a high degree of accuracy, for its truths and truthfulness have been demonstrated across history. Yes, repeatedly the Bible rises up to outlive its pallbearers.

As you read this book, I hope—like the author—that you will lay it down at some point to read the Book of Books. Might you find that the Bible is not only written to be read; rather, it reads us. How incredible that God has a personal interest in the struggles of our lives and has chosen to reveal Himself through the course of history in the pages of the Bible. Read on.

Ravi Zacharias
Author and speaker

Not everyone agrees with how the Bible came to us. The authorship of 1, 2, and 3 John is a good example. Scholars have debated whether these letters were written by the Apostle John or another person named John. This book will simply ascribe the authorship to "traditionally the Apostle John" and not report alternative theories. Such debates do not diminish the reliability of the Bible. The abundance of early evidence of the Bible's accuracy and authenticity—not a lack of such evidence—is what attracts study and speculation.

Except when using specific dates, this book will use the name of a century—"the fourteenth century" instead of "the 1300s," for instance. It can be confusing. The name of a century is taken from the year at the end of it. For instance, AD 1492 is in the fifteenth century.

English Bible translations mentioned and their abbreviations

ASV	American Standard Version
	Amplified Bible
	The Bishops' Bible
CEV	Contemporary English Version
	Cotton Patch Version
	The Coverdale Bible
	The Douay-Rheims Bible
ESV	English Standard Version
	The Geneva Bible
GNB	Good News Bible
	The Great Bible
KJV	King James Version
LB	The Living Bible
	The Matthew's Bible
	The Message: The Bible in Contemporary English
NASB	New American Standard Bible
NEB	New English Bible
NIV	New International Version
NKJV	New King James Version
NLT	New Living Translation
NRSV	New Revised Standard Version
	New World Translation
RSV	Revised Standard Version
RV	Revised Version
	The Taverner's Bible
TEV	Today's English Version
TNIV	Today's New International Version
	Tyndale Translation
	Wycliffe Translation
	Young's Literal Translation

INTRODUCTION

IS THE STORY OF THE BIBLE AN ACCOUNT OF ITS many translations? Is the story of the Bible part of the history of the Jewish people for more than three thousand years and the Christian church for two thousand years? Is the story of the Bible the effect it had on Western civilization? Is the story of the Bible the accounts of individuals whose lives were changed by its message?

The story of the Bible is all of that and more.

BIBLE TRANSLATION WAS A DANGEROUS BUSINESS in early sixteenth century England, largely because the Bible had become a symbol of the power struggle between the Church and those who wanted to reform it. Sir Thomas More spoke for many when he said it was heresy to think "we should believe nothing but plain Scripture" and let people read the Bible for themselves. This was not just a polite discussion. One hundred years earlier, some Lollards, a group that taught the authority of Scripture over the authority of the priests, had been burned alive with Bibles hung around their necks.

Nevertheless, William Tyndale translated the New Testament into English so that even "the boy that drives the plow in England" would be able to read and understand the Bible. The translation was condemned in 1526 and copies were burned in public. Ten years later Tyndale himself was betrayed, captured, and burned at the stake. But when boys who drove plows discovered for themselves what the Bible said, the nation was transformed. Within fifty years of Tyndale's death, "No greater moral change ever passed over a nation than passed over England. . . . England became a people of a book, and that book was the Bible."[1]

This passion for the Bible did not remain in England. Many who wanted religious freedom left England for America. "Mainly they were Christians who hoped to worship God with their whole lives, body, and soul; with a dazzling fervor that still lights up their journals, letters, and poetry 300 years later. . . . America was born in a passionate spiritual explosion. The explosion was created and fueled by the Bible."[2]

THROUGHOUT THE CENTURIES COUNTLESS ATTEMPTS have been made to suppress the Bible. But none has succeeded. It may seem strange in a day when Bibles are readily available in bookstores, in hotel rooms, and on the Internet that five hundred years ago William Tyndale was burned at the stake for the crime of publishing the New Testament in English.

The story of the Bible's writing, preservation, and translation is a fascinating one filled with intrigue, discovery, and adventure. In the end, though, Tyndale's dream—and that of Jerome, who translated the Bible into Latin; and of Martin Luther, who translated the Bible into German; and of Cameron Townsend, who founded Wycliffe Bible Translators—of the Bible's being available to everyone was a dream that changed the world. It was a dream that had a transforming effect on England and the English language. And it has had an effect on societies around the globe, from the most sophisticated to the most primitive, societies where people have been taught to read in their own language so that they can read the one book available to them—the Bible.

1 John Richard Green, *A Short History of the English People* (New York: Harper & Brothers, 1890), p. 460.
2 David Gelernter, "Bible Illiteracy in America," *The Weekly Standard*, May 23, 2005, Volume 010, Issue 34.

1

BEGINNINGS

(Right) John, the author of the fourth gospel, holds a codex, a format like a modern book. This picture is from a Greek New Testament completed in AD 1133 in the Byzantine monastery of Saint John the Baptist in Constantinople and now in the J. Paul Getty Museum in Los Angeles.

THE BIBLE IS A REMARKABLE COLLECTION OF BOOKS AND LETTERS. It was written in three languages by more than forty authors over a period of fifteen hundred years. Some of the writers were kings, some were poets, one was a physician, and another was a tax collector. Some parts of the New Testament were written by uneducated fishermen. In spite of this diversity, the Bible has one central, consistent theme: God made us, He loves us in spite of our naturally rebellious attitude toward Him, and He wants to reconcile us to Himself.

The Bible has two sections—the Old Testament and the New Testament. The word *testament* means a covenant or agreement between God and His people. The Old Testament tells the story of God's relationship with His chosen people, the Jews, from the time of the creation of the world to about 400 BC. The "agreement" between God and His people that was established at the time God gave the Ten Commandments to Moses—often called the Mosaic covenant—was one of Law. God gave the Jews rules to follow. The thirty-nine books that make up the Old Testament were recognized as Scripture by the Jews before the time of Christ and were translated into Greek in the third century BC, a translation called the Septuagint.

Ezra, the Old Testament scribe who led Jewish exiles in Babylon back to Israel in 458 BC, is shown writing in a codex and seated by a cupboard containing nine volumes. This image is a frontispiece of Codex Amiatinus, the earliest complete Vulgate Bible, which was created in a monastery in northeastern England as a gift for the pope in the eighth century. Codex Amiatinus is in the Biblioteca Medicea Laurenziana in Florence.

The New Testament tells the story of Jesus and his followers. Twenty-one of the twenty-seven books of the New Testament are letters that the apostles wrote after the death of Christ. While the Old Testament covenant of law led to the *conviction* of sin, the New Testament covenant of grace leads to the *forgiveness* of sins. (At the Last Supper, Jesus explained that the wine He gave to His disciples "is My blood of the new covenant, which is shed for many for the remission of sins."[3])

THE WORD "BIBLE" COMES FROM THE LATIN WORD *biblia* and the Greek word *biblos*, which mean simply *book*. This word might have come to mean *book* because the port of Byblos in modern Lebanon was where Egyptians exported to Greece the papyrus on which books and scrolls were written.

Papyrus, from which we get our word *paper*, was a tall reed plant that grew along the Nile River in Egypt, and was the same plant from which the basket was made that hid the infant Moses. (It is called "wicker" or "bulrushes" in English translations.) The manufacture of papyrus, the most important export of ancient Egypt, was controlled by the pharaohs and made by a carefully guarded process. "Without such a relatively cheap and convenient material, literature and the sciences could scarcely have developed as they did."[4] Although we don't know the Egyptian secret, we do know that papyrus can be made by cutting the inner parts of the stalks into long strips and soaking them in water long enough for decomposition to begin. The strips are then laid side by side and other strips placed on top at a right angle. The two layers are pressed and dried so that the strips adhere to each other. The papyrus sheet is then polished with a hard round object such as a stone or sea shell. The papyrus could be used either as sheets or connected in long strips and rolled around a stick to form a scroll. Various Bible translations use the words *scroll* and *book* interchangeably. In 2 Timothy 4:13 in the NIV, Paul asks Timothy to bring "my scrolls, especially the parchments," but in the NKJV, he says to bring "the books, especially the parchments."

Parchment was also used in ancient Egypt, but it became popular in the second century BC in Pergamum, a city in what is now Turkey, when King Ptolemy of Egypt refused to export papyrus to King Eumenes of Pergamum. Without a source of papyrus, the people of Pergamum perfected the manufacture of parchment by scraping and stretching the skins of animals—usually goat, sheep, or sometimes calf—into thin, paper-like sheets. Parchment was more durable than papyrus and easier to manufacture, and so it eventually replaced papyrus. Vellum, usually made from calf skin, is like parchment, but it is a finer quality of leather.

3 Matthew 26:28.
4 Roberts, C. H., "The Greek Papyri" in S. R. K. Glanville (ed.), *The Legacy of Egypt*, Oxford: Clarendon Press, 1963, 251.

Papyrus was made in ancient Egypt by cutting the inner part of the stalks into long strips (at left), soaking them in water, and laying them side by side (at right). They were then pressed, dried, and polished into individual sheets, which could be connected into a scroll.

Pergamum also developed the codex, a form that eventually replaced the scroll. In a scroll, which could be as long as thirty-five feet, words were written in columns on one side of the papyrus or parchment and rolled around a stick, which made it inconvenient to find easily a particular passage. A codex had words written on both sides of sheets, which were then folded and bound together. Modern books are codices, but the term is used only for handwritten manuscripts produced before the invention of printing. The name *Codex Vaticanus*, for instance, simply means that a particular manuscript in the Vatican library is in the form of a modern book instead of a scroll. The codex form was used much earlier by Christian scribes than by scribes of non-Christian literature.

THE BIBLE WAS WRITTEN IN THREE LANGUAGES. The Old Testament was written in Hebrew with small portions in Aramaic. The New Testament was written in Greek.

Hebrew and Aramaic are Semitic languages, a term derived from the name of Noah's oldest son, Shem. Arabic and Amharic (spoken in Egypt) are the two leading Semitic languages spoken today, with Hebrew and a number of other smaller Semitic languages also used in the Middle East and North Africa. Hebrew is written from right to left, and consists of a 22-symbol alphabet of only consonants.

The Gezer Calendar, a limestone tablet written about 1,000 BC, is the oldest existing example of the Hebrew language. It is probably a school child's exercise or perhaps the words to a song. (See sidebar on page 13.) Other examples of ancient Hebrew writing include (a) the Mesha Stele, also called the Moabite Stone (850 BC)—the Moabite King Mesha's account of his victories over Israel[5] written in Moabite, a Hebrew dialect; (b) the Samaritan Ostraca (750 BC)—sixty-five receipts for shipments of oil and wine written on broken pieces of pottery; (c) the Siloam Inscription (701 BC)—cursive Hebrew script carved into the wall of Hezekiah's tunnel in Jerusalem; and (d) the Lachish Letters (597 to 587 BC)—military correspondence related to Nebuchadnezzar's invasion of Israel, also written on broken pieces of pottery.

The primary source of information about classical Hebrew is the Old Testament itself, which means that if translators encounter a word that is used only once or twice in the Old Testament, there may not be other documents in which they can find that word to help determine its meaning. The most important discovery of Hebrew-language documents occurred in 1947, when Bedouin goatherds exploring a cliff-side cave near the Dead Sea found a cache of large earthen jars containing ancient scrolls and fragments that were more than two thousand years old. A few of the Dead Sea Scrolls were in Aramaic and Greek, but the rest were written in ancient Hebrew.

Aramaic was the language of the Assyrian, Babylonian, and Persian empires, all of which conquered Israel at one time or another. The Israelites began speaking Aramaic while they were in captivity, and over time Aramaic replaced Hebrew as their everyday language.

The use of Aramaic in the Old Testament is limited to the events in Nebuchadnezzar's court described in the book of Daniel, several sections of Ezra, one verse in Jeremiah, and a few other individual words. Jesus and His disciples spoke Aramaic, and the words *Abba*, *Maranatha*, and *Cephas* are all Aramaic, as is Jesus' reference to Psalm 22 while He was on the cross: "*Elí, Elí, lama sabachthani.*" However, while Aramaic was the language in which first-century Jews talked to one another, the language of commerce was Greek.

The oldest of any European language, Greek was spoken on the island of Crete as early as 1,400 BC and had several dialects, including Attic, which was spoken in Athens when it was in its glory. With the spread of Greek throughout the world due to Alexander the Great's conquests in the fourth century BC, however, a "common" Greek, called *Koine*, developed—a language in which the Persian merchant and Egyptian artisan might do business together. Even when Latin was made the official language of the Roman Empire, Greek remained the ordinary language of culture and commerce from western India to Egypt and Spain, in part because it was easy to learn and easy to write. Koine Greek brought significant changes to the vocabulary, pronunciation, and grammar of the more traditional dialects. Purists, who wanted to maintain the supremacy of the Greek of Plato and Plutarch, reacted strongly against

THE HEBREW ALPHABET

Hebrew has twenty-two consonants and no vowels. The reader has to determine by the context whether (in English, for instance) "MD" is *mad, med, mid, mod,* or *mud*. Hebrew is written from right to left and has only capital letters.

א	Aleph	silent
ב	Beth	B as in "boy" or V in "very"
ג	Gimel	G as in "go"
ד	Daleth	D as in "day"
ה	Hey	H as in "hat"
ו	Waw	W as in "way"
ז	Zayin	Z as in "zeal"
ח	Heth	CH as in "loch"
ט	Teth	T as in "toy"
י	Yod	Y as in "yet"
ך, כ	Kaph	K as in "keep" or KH as in "Bach"
ל	Lamed	L as in "let"
ם, מ	Mem	M as in "met"
ן, נ	Nun	N as in "net"
ס	Samekh	S as in "set"
ע	Ayin	silent
ף, פ	Pe	P as in "pet" or PH as in "phone"
ץ, צ	Tsadhe	TS as in "hits"
ק	Qoph	Q as in "oblique"
ר	Resh	R as in "run"
ש	Sin/Shin	S as in "so" or SH as in "shell"
ת	Taw	T as in "to"

Psalm 119 contains twenty-two sections of eight verses each, and each verse in a given section starts with the same Hebrew letter. Verse 1 through 8 all start with an aleph in Hebrew. Most English Bibles indicate the divisions by the Hebrew letter.

[5] 2 Kings 3:4-27.

THE GREEK ALPHABET

The Greek and Hebrew alphabets were both derived from the Phoenecian alphabet, but the Greeks added vowels, and so the alphabet has twenty-four letters. Greek contains both lowercase letters and capital letters and, like English, is written from left to right. Today Greek letters are used for many purposes. For instance the ratio of the diameter of a circle to its circumference (3.14159265) is called by the Greek letter *pi*.

CAPS	LOWERCASE		
Α	α	Alpha	A as in "father"
Β	β	Beta	B as in "boy"
Γ	γ	Gamma	G as in "got"
Δ	δ	Delta	D as in "dog"
Ε	ε	Epsilon	E as in "end"
Ζ	ζ	Zeta	ZD as in "Mazda"
Η	η	Eta	E as in "set"
Θ	θ	Theta	TH as in "thick"
Ι	ι	Iota	I as in "it"
Κ	ϰ	Kappa	K as in "sack"
Λ	λ	Lambda	L as in "light"
Μ	μ	Mu	M as in "mouse"
Ν	ν	Nu	N as in "nose"
Ξ	ξ	Xi	X as in "fox"
Ο	ο	Omicron	O as in "hop"
Π	π	Pi	P as in "pan"
Ρ	ϱ	Rho	R like a Spanish trilled R
Σ	σ, ς	Sigma	S as in "sister"
Τ	τ	Tau	T as in "stop"
Υ	υ	Upsilon	U as in French "une"
Φ	φ	Phi	PH as in "phone"
Χ	χ	Chi	CH as in Scottish "loch"
Ψ	ψ	Psi	PS as in "lips"
Ω	ω	Omega	O as in "grow"

Koine. But it was the language of everyday life and in many respects the first form of modern Greek. And Koine was the language of the New Testament.

Greek has an extraordinarily rich vocabulary and an ability, which English adapted, of constructing new words. *Biology*, for instance, is a compound of two Greek words: *bios*, meaning "life," and *logia*, meaning "study of." This richness and preciseness make Greek an ideal language for communicating both the story of the Gospels as well as the theological discussions of Paul and other New Testament writers.

THE GEZAR CALENDAR

About twenty miles west of Jerusalem, halfway to Tel Aviv, is Gezer, one of the most excavated sites in modern Israel. Joshua defeated the king of Gezer when the Israelites arrived in Canaan, but they "did not drive out the Canaanites."[6] Years later the Egyptian pharaoh destroyed Gezer and gave the city to Solomon as a dowry for marrying his daughter, and Solomon built up Gezer as a "storage city."

R.A. Stewart Macalister, a British archaeologist, made a number of important discoveries at Gezer, but his greatest find, which he made in 1908, was not a Canaanite city wall or the home of the governor—both of which he did discover—but a small, four-inch-tall soft limestone tablet listing the agricultural seasons and the appropriate farming activities. It reads:

Two months of harvest
Two months of planting
Two months are late planting
One month of hoeing
One month of barley-harvest
One month of harvest and festival
Two months of grape harvesting
One month of summer fruit

The tablet's message seems trivial; it was most likely a school child's exercise or a folk song or children's song. Its importance, however, is that the inscriptions are written in classic Hebrew in the tenth century BC—at the time of King Solomon, who had just received Gezer as a gift from Pharoah.

The Gezer Calendar, as the tablet has come to be known, is considered to be one of the earliest physical evidences of Hebrew writing. It is in the Museum of the Ancient Orient in Istanbul, Turkey.

[6] Joshua 16:10.

The Mesha Stele, also called the Moabite Stone, was discovered in 1868 in Dhiban, Jordan, the site of the ancient capital of Moab. The inscription of thirty-four lines tells of the victory of the Moabite King Mesha over "Omri king of Israel." Written in Moabite, a Hebrew dialect, it contains the earliest known reference to the name of God — YHWH. The monument, four feet tall and 31 inches wide, is in the Louvre in Paris.

WE DO NOT HAVE THE LETTERS PAUL ACTUALLY wrote, the Gospel in Matthew's handwriting, or any of what are called "original autographs" of the Bible. What we do have is more than 5,500 partial or complete ancient biblical manuscripts. These include about two thousand lectionary manuscripts, which were portions of Scriptures to be read in the church on holy days; more than 125 papyri, most of which date from the third and fourth centuries after Christ; three hundred or more uncials, which are manuscripts or fragments written in all capital letters, a style used before the ninth century AD; and more than 2,600 minuscules, later manuscripts written in a small, cursive Greek script that could be written more easily and quickly. Sir Frederic Kenyon, an authority on biblical manuscripts and former director of the British Museum, says that uncial manuscripts (the older ones) are "a very handsome form, and the early uncials, such as the Sinaiticus and Alexandrinus, are among the finest books in existence."

This remarkable abundance of ancient manuscripts and the fact that the oldest surviving New Testament manuscripts date to within seventy to 170 years from when they were first written makes the New Testament unique among ancient texts. For instance, the earliest existing manuscript of the writings of Virgil was copied 350 years after his death and it is the closest manuscript to the date of any author other than biblical writers. The earliest existing manuscripts of works by Aristotle and Sophocles were copied more than one thousand years after their authors' deaths. The existing manuscripts of writers of antiquity usually number in the dozens. The writings of Roman poets Virgil and Ovid are found in a few hundred existing manuscripts

THE BIBLE HAS ONE THEME: GOD MADE US, HE LOVES US in spite of our rebellious attitude toward Him, and He wants to reconcile us to Himself.

and fragments. The Bible is the only ancient writing with existing manuscripts in the thousands.

Of course, there are so many manuscripts because the Bible is not just another book. It is the Word of God to two of the world's great faiths—Judaism and Christianity. No one ever gave his life to translate and preserve the writings of Virgil or Homer. But many have dedicated their lives to the translation and preservation of the Bible. Moses told the Israelites that God wanted them to "lay up these words of mine in your heart and in your soul. . . . You shall teach them to your children, speaking of them when you sit

[7] Deuteronomy 11:18-19.
[8] A small box.

in your house, when you walk by the way, when you lie down, and when you rise up."[7] Even today, many Jews put a portion of Scripture in a mezuzah[8] on the doorpost of their house. For the past two thousand years Christians have copied, studied, preserved, and eventually translated portions of the Bible into thousands of languages around the world. And many died doing it, including William Tyndale in 1536 in exile in Antwerp and five American missionaries in 1956 on the bank of the Curaray River in Ecuador.

The story of the Bible is the story of the writing and preservation of the Hebrew Scriptures, including an amazing discovery of portions preserved for two thousand years near the Dead Sea. It is the story of the recognition of certain writings of the apostles as Scripture, of the persecution of Christians, and then—starting in 325—of the domination of Europe by the Christian church and the Bible through the Middle Ages. The story of the Bible includes the Bible's central role in the remarkable century from the time of the invention of printing with movable type to the Reformation. It is the story of the Bible's profound effect on Europe, particularly the United Kingdom, and how that nation's dedication to the Bible spread to America and eventually around the world.

Before the invention of the codex, Bibles were written as scrolls, a format still used in the traditional Hebrew Torah scroll. A Jewish scribe on Manhattan's Lower East Side repairs a Torah scroll.

THE CHALLENGE OF TRANSLATING HEBREW[9]

The ancient Hebrew language presents many challenges to a translator because it bears no resemblance to any European language. The fact that it was written from right to left makes it seem different, but that is not the greatest challenge.

Until the ninth and tenth centuries AD, Hebrew had no vowels and was sometimes written without spaces between words. In effect, ancient Hebrew was written to help recall to memory certain events, but the reader needed some knowledge of the contents before reading it. For instance, the first half of Psalm 23 from the King James Version (written from left to right) would look like this: (If you know Psalm 23, you will be reminded of it. But if you do not know it, you would have some difficulty figuring out the meaning.)

THLDSMSHPHRDSHLLNTWNT
HMKTHMTLDWNNGRNPSTRSHLDTHMBSDTHSTLLWTRS
HRSTRTHMSLHLDTHMNTHPTHSFRGHTSNSSFRHSNMSSK

In addition, some Hebrew words can no longer be translated with any certainty. For instance, Genesis 37:32 mentions that Jacob made for Joseph a *ketoneth passiym*. The first word is clearly *coat* or *tunic*. But the second word appears nowhere else in the Old Testament. It has been interpreted as a coat "of many colors," a coat "with long sleeves," a coat "with much embroidery," and even as a coat of "choice wool." The simple fact is that no one knows what the precise meaning of *passiym* is, and there is no way we can find out.

Finally the word order in the typical Hebrew sentence was very different from English, and Hebrew has no verb tenses. Past, present, and future tenses do not exist in Hebrew.

Some characteristics of the language, however, make translation easier. Old Testament Hebrew is known for its simple, direct style and a vivid imagery. God's anger is described in one passage as "redness of the nostrils," the keel of a ship is its "backbone," and the shore of a sea is its "lip." Another characteristic is that Hebrew poetry is not based on rhyme but on parallelism, in which two lines repeat the same idea. Isaiah 1:4, for instance, contains three lines that repeat the same concept:

Alas, sinful nation,
A people laden with iniquity,
A brood of evildoers

Proverbs 10:1 is an example of antithetical parallelism:

A wise son makes a glad father,
But a foolish son is the grief of his mother.

Because Hebrew presents such unusual challenges for modern translators, the study of early translations of the Old Testament such as the Greek Septuagint is important because they help us understand what early translators thought the Hebrew meant.

[9] Adapted from *The Bible Almanac*, ed. James I. Packer, Merrill C. Tenney, and William White, Jr. (Nashville: Thomas Nelson, 1980), 343–45.

2

THE PEOPLE OF THE BOOK

(Right) *The Dead Sea Scrolls, found in caves including those in these cliffs, contain nearly the entire Hebrew Bible in manuscripts that are one thousand years older than those previously available. In front of the caves is the Wadi Qumran, which leads to the Dead Sea about a mile to the east. Behind the caves on the plateau are the excavated remains of the Qumran Community.*

THE SUMARIAN CITY OF UR WAS THE largest city in the world four thousand years ago.

Built near the place where the Tigris and Euphrates rivers emptied into the Persian Gulf about two hundred miles southeast of modern Baghdad,[10] Ur was the sacred city of Nanna, the moon god, whose temple included a ziggurat, a huge stepped platform that was partially restored under Iraq's Suddam Hussein in the 1980s. The royal tombs at Ur, discovered in the 1920s, were filled with extravagant gold and lapis lazuli jewelry, gold and silver cups, alabaster bowls, and art objects that opened the world's eyes to the glory of ancient Sumeria. King Ur-Nammu is credited with writing the oldest existing code of laws. The Sumerian creation story, the world's oldest, includes a description of a flood that destroyed all people and animals except those saved in a huge boat. The city of Ur was amazingly cultured, sophisticated, and powerful.

Living in Ur[11] shortly after the completion of the ziggurat was a man whose father, Terah, "served other gods,"[12] most likely Nanna. This man, Abraham, was told by God to leave Ur and move his family on a twelve hundred-mile journey to a new land.[13] "I will make you a great nation; I will bless you and make your name great," God promised. "And in you all the families of the earth shall be blessed."[14] The new land was Canaan (modern Israel), and it was there that God would establish Abraham's descendants (the Jewish people), who would bless all the families of the earth through the birth of the Messiah. In addition, it was through the Jewish people that God gave His Word to the world.[15]

10 Today, because of changing seas, the ruins of Ur are well inland.
11 Some scholars think that Abraham's birthplace was not Ur, but Urfa, near Haran, in modern Turkey.
12 Joshua 24:2.
13 See Acts 7:2-4.
14 Genesis 12:2-3.
15 See Romans 3:1-2.

The Ziggurat in Ur, a massive 210 feet by 150 feet, was built about the same time Abraham was born in Ur—between 2100 and 2000 BC. Nanna, the moon god, was said to live here, and the ziggurat included a small "bedchamber of the god" on the top. The ziggurat was excavated in the 1920s and 1930s by Sir Leonard Woolley, and in 1985 Saddam Hussein ordered part of the façade and the monumental staircase to be rebuilt using bricks bearing his name.

Abraham and his family left Ur between 2100 and 2000 BC and traveled to Haran in modern Turkey, where they stayed until Terah died. Abraham then left Haran when he was seventy-five years old and traveled on to Canaan.

About two hundred years after Abraham and his family arrived in Canaan, Joseph, Abraham's great-grandson, was sold to traders on their way to Egypt by his own brothers. Joseph became second in command to Pharaoh, and when a famine hit Canaan, his entire family moved to Egypt where they grew into the Hebrew nation.

When "another king arose who did not know Joseph," the Hebrews were made slaves until, in 1446 BC,[16] Moses, an Israelite who had grown up and been educated as an adopted son of Pharaoh's daughter, led all the Israelites[17] out of Egypt, through the Sinai Desert for forty years, and back to Canaan. This same Moses is the traditional author of the Pentateuch, the first five books of the Bible. Although nowhere does the text itself claim him to be the writer, it does mention six times when Moses wrote something, including the "Book of the Law," which was kept with the ark of the covenant.[18] His authorship of the Pentateuch means that Moses penned more of the Bible than anyone else.

The Old Testament is a collection of thirty-nine books believed to be inspired by God and written by numerous writers over the course of more than one thousand years. It includes historical accounts of the nation of Israel, poetry of the psalms, and prophetic proclamations to obey God. The English Bible groups the Old Testament into four sections: the Pentateuch (five books, Genesis to Deuteronomy), History (twelve books, Joshua to Esther), Poetry and Wisdom (five books, Job to the Song of Solomon) and the Prophets (seventeen books, Isaiah to Malachi). The Jews organized the same Scriptures into twenty-two or twenty-four books in three divisions: the Law, the Prophets, and the Writings. The difference is the arrangement. The English Bible, for instance, has twelve separate books written by the "minor prophets," whereas the Hebrew Scriptures puts them all in a single book.

The first five books, the Pentateuch, tell the story of God's creation of the world, the first man and woman's fall from God's favor in the garden of Eden, the Flood, the call of Abraham, and the history of the descendants of Abraham's grandson Jacob—whose name was changed by God to Israel—until the Jewish people became a nation in Egypt and escaped under the leadership of Moses. The Pentateuch tells of God's giving the Ten Commandments at Mount Sinai, the establishment of the Mosaic covenant, and the development of a system of worship in the tabernacle.

The twelve books of history continue the story begun in the Pentateuch. The Jewish nation entered

16 Some scholars believe it was about 1290 BC.

17 Numbers 12:37 says 600,000 plus women and children.

18 Deuteronomy 31:24 ff.

Canaan, the land God promised to Abraham, and went through seven cycles. First they were in servitude to a foreign nation, then they cried out to God, God gave the people peace through the leadership of a judge, and then the next cycle began with a foreign nation again placing Israel in servitude. During the time of Samuel, the last judge, the people demanded a king, and so God anointed Saul, then David, and finally Solomon as kings. The reigns of David and Solomon were the height of Israel's glory, and after Solomon's death in 931 BC, the nation divided into the northern kingdom, called Israel, and the southern kingdom, called Judah.

BEFORE THE DISCOVERY of the Dead Sea Scrolls, the earliest known manuscripts of the Old Testament were not Hebrew, but copies of the Greek Septuagint.

None of the kings of the northern kingdom were godly men, and in 722 BC the Assyrians (who came from what is now roughly Iran and Iraq) captured the northern kingdom, took the people into captivity, and for the most part the Israelites never returned to the Promised Land. The kings of the southern kingdom, however, were a mixed bag—some "did evil in the sight of the Lord" and others "did what was right in the eyes of the Lord." But in 586 BC the Babylonians, who had become more powerful than the Assyrians, captured Judah and took the leading citizens into exile. Over the next nearly 150 years, there were three returns of Jews from Babylon to their land: in 536 BC under the leadership of Zerubbabel, in 458 BC under the leadership of Ezra, and in 444 BC under the leadership of Nehemiah. The Old Testament history ends with Nehemiah going back to Persia (which by this time had defeated Babylon) and then returning again to Jerusalem to find that some of the Jewish men had married foreign women and that their children could not even speak Hebrew.

The third section of the Old Testament is poetry and Wisdom Literature: Job, Psalms, Proverbs, Ecclesiastes, and Song of Solomon. Much of this part of the Bible is identified with historical events. King David, for instance, wrote many of the psalms, and Solomon is the traditional author of most of the last three of these five books. These Old Testament books all reflect the human heart and its encounter

Black-skinned and yellow-skinned prisoners of war from Nubia (a region along the Nile in southern Egypt and northern Sudan) and Syro-Palestine make bricks for the Temple of Amun at Karnak. Although the light-skinned workers cannot be identified as Israelites, the picture illustrates Exodus 1:13-14: "So the Egyptians made the children of Israel serve with rigor. And they made their lives bitter with hard bondage—in mortar, in brick." The picture is from the tomb of Rekhmire (ca. 1470-1445 BC).

According to a letter describing the translation of the Septuagint, after King Ptolemy of Egypt brought 72 Jewish elders to Alexandria, he held a seven-day banquet where he asked them questions and was astonished by their wisdom. The king, attended by two servants, reclines at the left. According to the description accompanying this picture, the elders also reclined, but the artist did not picture them that way. The picture is from an 11th-century Octateuch (the Pentateuch plus Joshua, Judges, and Ruth) in the Vatican Library.

with God, with sin, and with the issues of life. We can identify closely with these because the human heart has not changed in the last three thousand years.

The final section of the Old Testament consists of seventeen books written by men who communicated God's message courageously. Some prophesied to people in the northern kingdom of Israel; others to those in the southern kingdom of Judah. Eleven prophesied before the people to whom they spoke were taken into captivity; Ezekiel and Daniel wrote during their own captivity in Babylon; Haggai, Zechariah, and Malachi prophesied after they returned from exile. A tremendous variety exists in the personalities and writing styles of the prophets, but they tended to have four themes: (a) the prophets exposed the sinful practices of the people; (b) they called the people back to the moral, civil, and ceremonial law of God, reminding the people about the character of God and urging them to trust Him with all their hearts; (c) they warned of coming judgment; and (d) they anticipated the coming Messiah. Malachi was the last book of the Old Testament to be written, between 433 and 420 BC.

Between about 300 and 30 BC some writings were added to the Old Testament that collectively are called by Protestants and Jews the Apocrypha, a word meaning "hidden" or "secret things," and by Catholics the deuterocanonical books.[19] These are historically and culturally interesting writings, and when the Old Testament was first translated into Greek, most of them were included. Some of the early church fathers accepted part or all of these writings as Scripture, but others, including Jerome, whose translation of the Bible into Latin was considered the most authoritative by the Roman Church, did not. One reason is that neither Jesus nor the apostles ever referred to any of these books. When Martin Luther translated the Bible into German in 1534, he put the Apocrypha in a separate section between the Old and New Testaments because he did not consider these books to be Scripture. In response, the Council of Trent declared in 1546 that the deuterocanonical books were part of Scripture. The historic Protestant and Jewish position, however, is that they are not Scripture.

THE OLD TESTAMENT WAS WRITTEN IN HEBREW, and as long as the Jews spoke Hebrew there was no need for translations. However, the Jewish people were influenced by the Assyrians, Babylonians, Greeks,

[19] Various writings have been included in the Apocrypha. Luther's Bible has seven books plus additions to Esther and Daniel. The New English Bible has twelve books, plus additions to Esther and Daniel. There are seven Catholic deuterocanonical books – Tobias, Judith, Wisdom, Ecclesiasticus, Baruch, 1 Maccabees, and 2 Maccabees – plus additions to Esther and two additions to Daniel: The Story of the Three Children and the stories of Susanna and the Elders and of Bel and the Dragon.

[20] The word *Septuagint* is Latin for *seventy* and is often referred to as the LXX, the Roman numerals for the number seventy.

Persians, and Romans, and by the beginning of the third century BC, knowledge of Hebrew was becoming lost, and with it the ability to read or understand the Word of God. As a result the Jews translated their Scriptures into Greek and Aramaic.

The oldest and most important translation of the Old Testament, called the Septuagint,[20] was in Greek and was begun in the third century BC in Alexandria, the capital of Egypt. The story of the translation was told in a letter claiming to be written by an official in the court of the Egyptian King Ptolemy II Philadelphus at the time the king ordered the translation. It is now thought that the letter was written one hundred years later, but the story has been repeated often enough to achieve legendary status and to be embellished. According to this letter, Ptolemy wanted copies of all known books in his library, including the Hebrew Scriptures, and so he had seventy-two scholarly Jews brought from Jerusalem to Alexandria to translate the Old Testament into Greek. The translation of the Pentateuch was miraculously made in seventy-two days. Each translator—or pair of translators, depending on which version of the story you read—working independently produced seventy-two (or thirty-six) identical translations. Translation of the entire Old Testament into Greek actually took two centuries.

The Septuagint is important because of its wide use and because it became an authoritative Greek-language source for two thousand years of translations of the Old Testament into other languages. Before the discovery of the Dead Sea Scrolls, the earliest known manuscripts of the Old Testament were not Hebrew, but copies of the Greek Septuagint. The Septuagint was the Scripture of the

METICULOUS JEWISH SCRIBES

Before the invention of the printing press, every copy of every manuscript had to be made by hand—painstakingly page after page, line after line, word after word. Errors could be introduced if the copy was not made carefully, and so the Jews developed rules for preventing scribal errors in scrolls used in the synagogue.

- Each day a scribe would make sure his reed pen was writing well by dipping it in ink and writing the name *Amalek* and then crossing it out.[21]
- All materials had to be made according to strict specifications. Parchments had to be made from the skins of clean (kosher) animals and quills made from feathers of clean birds. The ink must be black and prepared according to scribal specifications.
- No word or even a letter could be written from memory. A scribe must have another scroll open before him and pronounce every word out loud before copying it.
- Before writing the name of God, a scribe must reverently wipe his pen and say, "I am writing the name of God for the holiness of His name."
- Every letter had to have some space around it. If one letter touched another or if a letter was defective because of incorrect writing, a hole, a tear, or a smudge so that it could not be easily read, the scroll was invalidated.
- Each column must have no fewer than forty-eight nor more than sixty lines and must be exactly like the manuscript being copied.
- Within thirty days of completion, an editor would review the manuscript, counting every letter and every word as a way of checking. The editor would also make sure that the middle word on each page of the copy was the same as the middle words on the manuscript being copied.
- Up to three mistakes on any page could be corrected within thirty days. If more mistakes were found or if mistakes were not fixed within thirty days, the entire manuscript had to be buried. If a single letter was added or a single letter left out, the manuscript had to be fixed or buried.

In case you were wondering, the Torah (Pentateuch) has 304,805 letters and 79,976 words in Hebrew.

[21] See Deuteronomy 25:19 for the background of this practice.

When Jewish zealots tried to repel the Romans from Jerusalem, Titus, who later became a Roman emperor, surrounded the city in AD 70. Eventually a fire started when a Roman soldier threw a burning stick onto one of the temple's walls. It destroyed the temple and much of the city. Very few manuscripts survived the fire. The Roman emperor Domitian later honored his brother Titus by building an arch in Rome that included a relief showing Roman soldiers carrying spoils from the temple.

early Christian church, and when New Testament writers quoted the Old Testament, they usually quoted the Septuagint. Even today the twenty-three-hundred-year-old Septuagint is the Old Testament text used by the Greek Orthodox Church.

The Septuagint was also part of a massive edition of the Old Testament prepared by the great Christian scholar Origen in the first half of the third century AD. The Hexapla contained six Old Testament versions in parallel columns: Hebrew, Hebrew transliterated into Greek characters, the Septuagint, and three other Greek translations all made in the second century. The complete Hexapla may have never been produced because of its size, and it exists today only in fragments.

The Old Testament was also translated into Aramaic in what are called "targums," which were interpretations of Scripture rather than literal translations. Different targums on the same passage would offer different comments. "All translations of the Bible are necessarily interpretive to some extent, but the Targums differ in that they are interpretive as a matter of policy, and often to an extent that far exceeds the bounds of translation or even paraphrase."[22]

Syriac was a dialect of Aramaic spoken by people to the east of Israel, and missionaries took Syriac as far east as India. About two hundred years after Christ, the Old Testament was translated into Syriac, but unlike other Old Testament translations, the Syriac translation was made from Hebrew and not from the Greek Septuagint. Another early translation of the Old Testament was Coptic, a language spoken by people in Egypt.

DETERMINING WHICH WRITINGS CONSTITUTE THE Word of God and thus are part of Scripture is called identifying the "canon" of Scripture. Derived from the Greek word *kanon*, meaning "rule" or "standard of measure," a canon is the accepted or official version of something. The canon of Scripture refers to those writings that are authoritative for faith and practice because they are divinely inspired.

To be part of Scripture a book must be inspired by God. From a practical standpoint the primary criterion for canonicity was the author's relationship with God—was he a genuine prophet, speaking God's words? Was the message of the book consistent with earlier revelations from God?

No one questioned that Moses spoke God's words,[23] and so the five books of the Pentateuch were accepted as Scripture long before other books of the Old Testament. In fact, the Samaritans say that only the Pentateuch is Scripture. (See sidebar on page 27.) The Prophets were accepted next as canonical, and the Writings last. By the third century BC, when the Septuagint was translated, the books of the Old Testament as we know them today had been identified

22 Bruce Metzger, "Important Early Translations of the Bible," *Bibliotheca Sacra* 150 (January-March 1993), 42.
23 See John 9:29.
24 Bruce Metzger, *An Introduction to the Apocrypha* (Oxford: Oxford University Press, 1957), 8.
25 Deuteronomy 6:4.

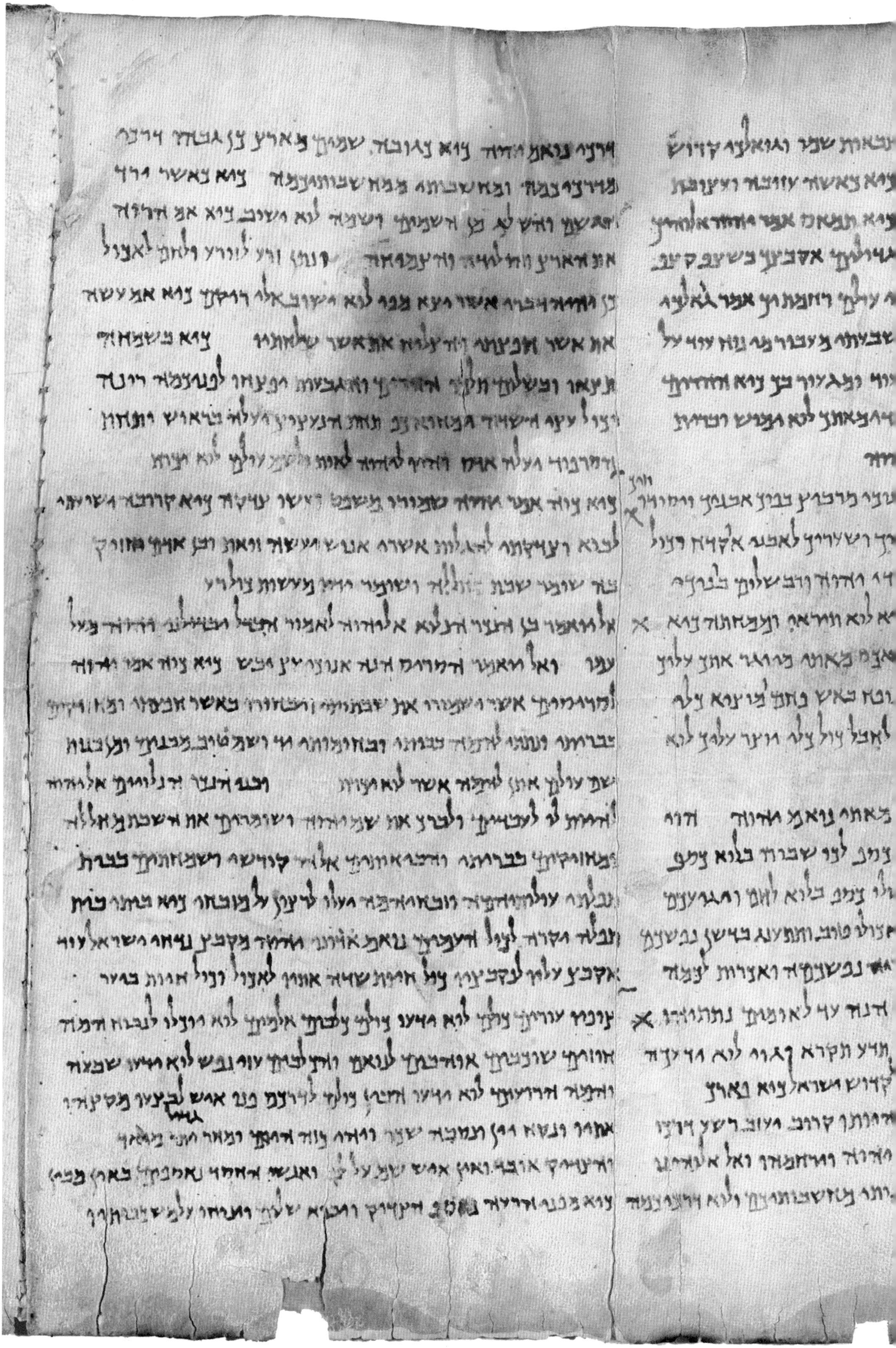

AH SCROLL

croll is the Great Isaiah Scroll,
nmed Ahmed el-Hamed and
ohn Trever. The Great Isaiah
xt of Isaiah and is 24 feet long,
4 columns of text on seventeen

iah Scroll you are holding is
g (from right to left) columns
(Isaiah 54:4–55:8), and 46
ne in the right-hand column is
o has believed our report? And
rd been revealed?" The seventh
ds with "He is despised and
ows and acquainted with grief."

st century BC, and except for a
tical to the text of Isaiah in the
w manuscript from AD 850.

entire Great Isaiah Scroll at
ter/Isaiah_Scrolling/index.html.

rmission. Photo © Israel Museum, Jerusalem.

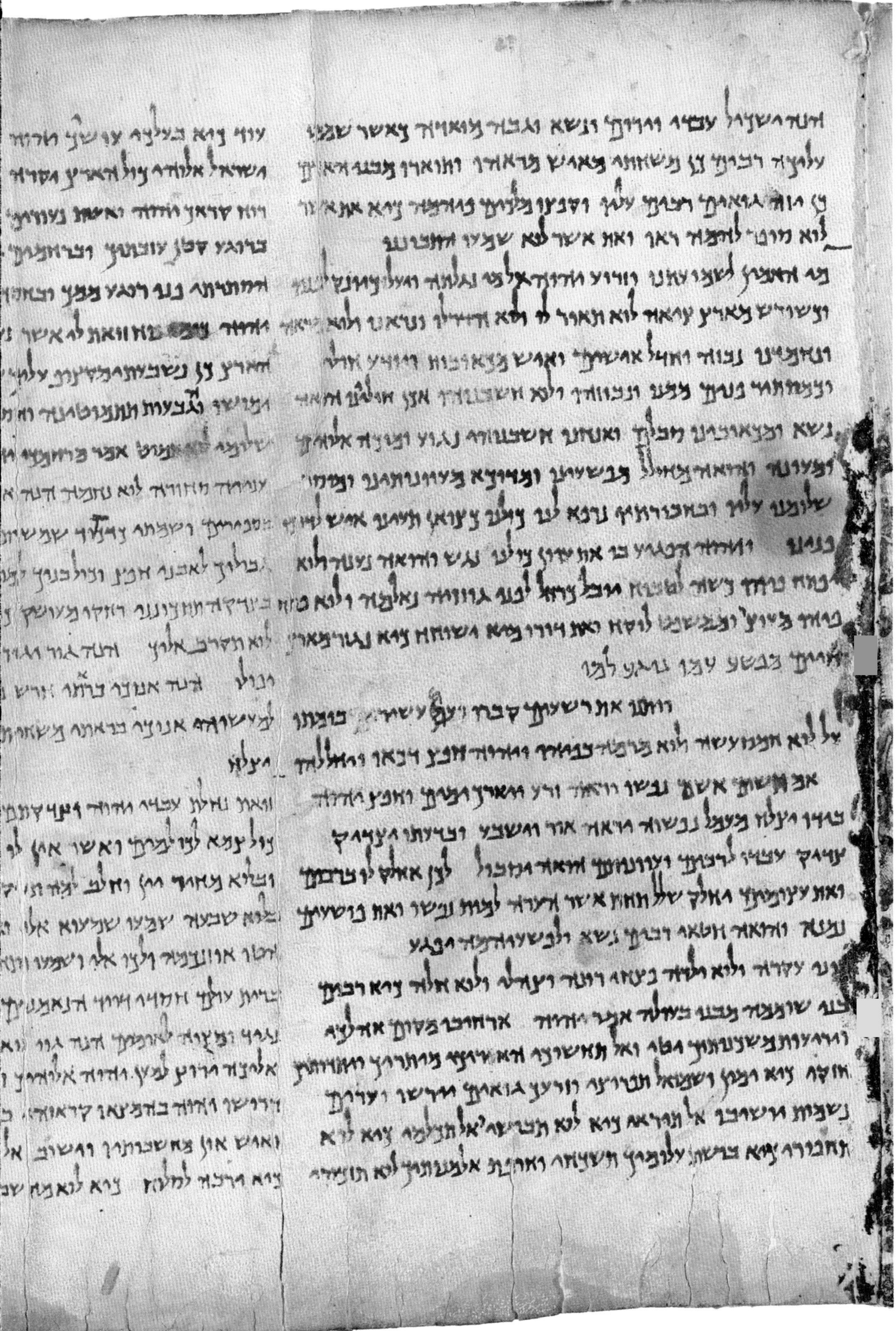

GREAT ISAI

The only complete Dead Sea S
discovered in 1947 by Muha
pictured on page 25, held by
Scroll contains the complete te
about 11 inches high, and has 5
strips of leather sewn together.

The portion of the Great Is
the fourteenth strip containin
44 (Isaiah 52:13–54:4), 45
(Isaiah 55:8–57:2). The fifth li
the beginning of Isaiah 53: "Wh
to whom has the arm of the Lo
line in the right column er
rejected by men, A Man of sorr

This scroll was written in the fi
few scribal errors its text is ide
oldest previously known Hebre

You can view and unroll the
http://www.imj.org.il/shrine_cer

Courtesy of The Israel Museum and used by p

as Scripture. When the first-century historian Josephus wrote about Judaism in *Against Apion*, he reported that the Jews have "twenty-two books [corresponding to our thirty-nine in English], which contain the records of all the past times; which are justly believed to be divine." Josephus also felt that after about 400 BC "there has not been an exact succession of prophets since that time."

Very few manuscripts survived the Roman Army's siege of Jerusalem in AD 70 when the temple and city were destroyed. With their center of worship gone and Christianity spreading, Jewish leaders under Rabbi Johanan ben Zakkai realized that the preservation of their Scriptures was important to the Jewish national unity and identity, and so they founded a school of Jewish law in Jamnia, a town near the Mediterranean Sea south of Joppa. In about AD 100 a council of these Jewish leaders drew up a list of accepted books of Scripture, which were the same Old Testament books Josephus mentioned and the ones we have today. The Apocrypha was not included. The Council of Jamnia did not decide the Hebrew canon; instead the council confirmed "what the most spiritually sensitive souls in Judaism had been accustomed to regard as being Scripture."[24] This council also drew up rules to make sure that copies of those Scriptures would be transmitted accurately, one of which was that when a copy had been made of an old manuscript that was worn or tattered, the old manuscript would be buried or destroyed. This is why, except for a few fragments, no Hebrew manuscripts from before AD 850 existed—until an amazing discovery in 1947.

His authorship of the Pentateuch means that Moses penned more of the Bible than anyone else. This statue by Michelangelo in Rome shows Moses with horns, possibly because Jerome's Latin translation in Exodus 34:29 describes Moses as having horns after he talked with God, instead of saying "the skin of his face shone."

PRIOR TO 1947 THE ONLY MANUSCRIPT PORTION of Hebrew Scripture from before the time of Christ was the Nash Papyrus. Acquired from an Egyptian antiquities dealer in 1898, it consists of four small fragments with twenty-four lines of Hebrew text containing the Ten Commandments and the Shema ("Hear, O Israel: The Lord our God, the Lord is one!"[25]). Thought to have been part of a scroll used in worship and dated to the first or second centuries BC, the Nash Papyrus is in the Cambridge University Library in England. Except for this one papyrus, there was a period of more than one thousand years between the writing of the last book of the Old Testament and the earliest Hebrew manuscript. This lack of ancient Hebrew manuscripts raised the question of how faithfully the Old Testament had been transmitted.

Although ancient copies of the Hebrew Old Testament did not exist, there were early copies of the Septuagint and the Samaritan Pentateuch. The oldest existing Old Testament manuscripts, therefore, were part of Bibles used by Christians, the most significant of which are listed here.

The first Dead Sea Scrolls were discovered in early 1947 and sold that summer to Metropolitan Samuel (middle) who spent six months trying to determine their significance. In February 1948, Samuel's friend, Father Butrus Sowmy (left, holding the Habakkuk Commentary), took them to the American School of Oriental Research in Jerusalem where scholar and photographer John Trever (right, holding the Great Isaiah Scroll) recognized their importance and asked Sowmy to bring them back so that he could photograph them. On February 21, 1948, in addition to taking the first photos of the Dead Sea Scrolls made for scholarly study, Trever had this photo made.

THE CHESTER BEATTY PAPYRI - In 1930 and 1931 Chester Beatty, an American collector who had made a fortune in copper mining, purchased some papyri from an antiquities dealer in Egypt. The University of Michigan also purchased fragments from the same codex about the same time. One story is that these papyri were found in urns in an Egyptian Coptic Christian cemetery. Seven of these eleven manuscripts contain portions of eight Old Testament books in Greek: Genesis, Esther, Isaiah, Jeremiah, Ezekiel, and Daniel are from the third century; Numbers and Deuteronomy are thought to have been copied between AD 120 and 150. At the time they were discovered, these manuscripts were the earliest known copies of Old Testament books. They are primarily in the Chester Beatty Library in Dublin, Ireland and at the University of Michigan.[26]

CODEX VATICANUS - In the Vatican Library since 1475, this codex dates to the first half of the fourth century and is the oldest nearly complete copy of the Greek Bible in existence.

CODEX SINAITICUS - Dating to about AD 350, it was discovered in 1844 in a monastery at Mount Sinai and contains about half of the Old Testament in Greek and the complete New Testament.

CODEX ALEXANDRINUS - Dating to about AD 425, this codex consists of 773 parchment leaves with most of the Old and New Testaments in Greek.

CODEX EPHRAEMI - Dating to about AD 450, this is a parchment copy of the Septuagint that was washed off so the pages could be reused for the sermons of Ephraem, a Syrian theologian and hymn writer. With much effort the original Septuagint can be read.[27]

In 1936 Sir Frederic Kenyon wrote, "We must accept the fact that for the Old Testament there is a gap of more than a thousand years between our earliest Hebrew manuscript and the latest of the books contained in it. . . . Since about the year AD 100 [the text of the Old Testament] has been handed down with no substantial variation; but before that period . . . to recover the original form we must depend mainly on the Septuagint."[28] Eleven years later the accuracy of that statement changed dramatically.

FROM JERUSALEM TO THE DEAD SEA IS FEWER THAN fifteen miles, but the two are worlds apart. Jerusalem is nearly 2,700 feet *above* sea level; at 1,300 feet *below* sea level, the Dead Sea is the lowest spot on earth. Very soon after leaving Jerusalem, the traveler passes

26 See also page 33.
27 See also page 33.
28 Frederic Kenyon, *The Story of the Bible* (Grand Rapids: Eerdmans Publishing Co., 1967), p. 11, 13.
29 William Foxwell Albright, personal communication to Metropolitan Athanasius Samuel, March 15, 1948.

When he was about 13, Muhammed Ahmed el-Hamed—pictured here in 1966 with his wife and five children—left his two sleeping cousins early one morning, climbed 350 feet to a cave they had seen two days earlier, and went exploring. All he found was broken pottery and a number of narrow jars—nothing of value, he thought. Nevertheless, he apparently took with him the Great Isaiah Scroll, the Habakkuk Commentary, and the Manual of Discipline.

Bethany, where Mary and Martha and Lazaraus lived, and then enters the Judean Wilderness where Saint George's Monastery, founded in the fifth century, clings to the mountainside by a deep gorge called Wadi Kelt. The area by the northeastern shore of the Dead Sea is mountainous, barren, and rocky.

In early 1947 young Bedouin shepherds, looking for a stray sheep or goat, climbed the cliffs near the Dead Sea. The story they told is that Muhammed Ahmed el-Hamed threw a stone into one of the caves on the side of the cliff, thinking that he would frighten the animal. Instead, he heard the breaking of pottery. Later, in the dark and smelly cave he found jars containing ancient scrolls wrapped in linen. It was the greatest manuscript discovery of modern times.[29]

The seven scrolls the boys (or perhaps others—much of archaeology contains a bit of cloak-and-dagger intrigue and details are sometimes unclear) removed from that cave included the Great Isaiah Scroll, the oldest complete biblical manuscript ever discovered. Eventually dated to the first century BC, this scroll contains all sixty-six chapters of the book of Isaiah and, except for some minor scribal errors, its text is identical to the text of Isaiah in the oldest Hebrew manuscript in existence until that time from AD 850. Here was dramatic evidence that the transmission of the Old Testament text had been done faithfully. In addition to the Isaiah scroll, the cave contained a commentary on the first two chapters of Habakkuk, a collection of hymns or psalms, and a "Manual of Discipline" for those who wanted to join the Qumran community that had hidden the scrolls.

The Bedouin boys took their finds to a Bethlehem antiquities dealer named Kando, who sold four of the scrolls to the Syrian Orthodox Archbishop of Jerusalem, Metropolitan Athanasius Samuel, for about $250. In November, on the same day that the United Nations voted to create a Jewish state for the first time in two thousand years, another Bethlehem antiquities dealer sold the remaining three scrolls to an archaeology professor at Hebrew University named Eleazer Lipa Sukenik, who carried them back to Jerusalem in a paper bag.

Archbishop Samuel wanted to sell his four scrolls to raise money for Palestinian refugees, but when he failed to find a buyer, he took them to the United States where they were displayed at the Library of Congress. Meanwhile five other caves near the first one were explored, other fragments found, and the buildings of the community at Qumran were

The Great Isaiah Scroll, the Temple Scroll, the Manual of Discipline, and other Dead Sea Scrolls are housed in the unique Shrine of the Book in Jerusalem. The museum opened in 1965 and was built as a repository for the first seven scrolls found in 1947.

discovered on a dry plateau about a mile from the shore of the Dead Sea. Excavation began in 1951.

On June 1, 1954, Metropolitan Samuel placed an ad in *The Wall Street Journal*:

> "The Four Dead Sea Scrolls"
>
> Biblical Manuscripts dating back to at least 200 BC are for sale. This would be an ideal gift to an educational or religious institution by an individual or group. Box F 206, *The Wall Street Journal*.

The four scrolls were purchased for $250,000 on behalf of the state of Israel by Yagael Yadin, a great archaeologist and son of Eleazer Sukenik, who had bought the other original three scrolls, but Yadin did not let Metropolitan Samuel know who was really buying them. Now all seven of the intact Dead Sea Scrolls were in the hands of the Israeli government, which built the Shrine of the Book, a museum in Jerusalem, to house them.

The community at Qumran was probably Essene Jews, who had lived there since about 150 BC. It is thought that when the Romans began persecuting the Jews about AD 66, the people at Qumran hid their library in caves in the surrounding hills. More than nine hundred documents have been found, representing 350 separate works, and tens of thousands of fragments. The caves yielded copies of nonbiblical texts, apocryphal works, and copies of every book of the Old Testament except Esther and the Song of Solomon.

A particularly intriguing find made in 1952 in Cave 3 is a copper scroll containing a list of sixty-four places where sacred objects and huge quantities of gold and silver were hidden. This list probably describes the treasures of the Jerusalem temple that were buried shortly before the Romans destroyed the city. Some of the locations seem very specific, such as, "In the funerary shrine, in the third course of stones: 100 gold ingots." But because the landmarks are unknown today, they are not specific enough for anyone to find the treasure estimated to be worth at least one billion dollars.

Controversy has surrounded the Dead Sea Scrolls, both in their interpretation and in a failure to make them available to scholars in a timely fashion. The scrolls are significant in what they tell us about the history of Judaism and about the development of early Christianity. But for our purposes their significance is in what they tell us about the transmission of the Hebrew Bible. For one thing, for two thousand years great reliance had been given to the Greek Septuagint, but how do we know that the Septuagint was an accurate translation of the third-century BC Hebrew? A comparison of the Dead Sea Scrolls with the Septuagint gives us an answer: the Septuagint translators faithfully translated the Hebrew text.

The Dead Sea Scrolls have given us nearly the entire Hebrew Bible in manuscripts that are one thousand years older than those previously available. The Dead Sea Scrolls provide astonishing confirmation that the Old Testament Scripture we have today is virtually the same as that being read a few centuries before Christ. The accuracy of the transmission is remarkable!

THE SAMARITAN PENTATEUCH

The Samaritans and Jews did not get along.

In 722 BC the Assyrians invaded the northern kingdom of Israel and brought with them foreign (pagan) people who intermarried with the tribes of Ephraim and Manasseh. According to the first-century historian Josephus, their descendants were the Samaritans. The Samaritans worshiped Jehovah, but when the Jewish leaders who returned to Jerusalem from Babylon refused to let the Samaritans take part in rebuilding the temple in Jerusalem, the Samaritans became bitterly hostile toward the Jews. In the fourth century BC the Samaritans built a temple on Mount Gerizim, about thirty miles north of Jerusalem, and said that Gerizim, not Jerusalem, was the only place to worship God.

Jews considered Samaritans apostates and idolaters and called them "that foolish people that dwell in Shechem."[30] The Samaritans considered the Jews apostate because the center of their worship was Jerusalem. The animosity between the Jews and Samaritans increased when the Jewish Maccabean leader John Hyrcanus destroyed the Samaritan temple on Mount Gerizim in 128 BC. By the time of Jesus, it was common knowledge that "Jews have no dealings with Samaritans."[31]

The Samaritans accepted only the Pentateuch (Genesis, Exodus, Leviticus, Numbers, and Deuteronomy) as Scripture and not any of the other books of the Old Testament. In the second century BC they made their own copy of the Pentateuch in Hebrew. The earliest surviving copies of the Samaritan Pentateuch are from the Middle Ages, but the close correlation of these manuscripts with the Jewish Masoretic text and the Dead Sea Scrolls is one more confirmation of the accuracy of the text of the first five books of the Old Testament.

Today there is still a Samaritan community of fewer than one thousand people, some living in Nablus near Mount Gerizim in the West Bank and some living in the Israeli town of Holon near Tel Aviv.

30 Ecclesiasticus 50:25-26.
31 John 4:9.

3

FOUNDATION OF A NEW FAITH

THE OLD AND NEW TESTAMENTS FORM ONE STORY. JESUS TOLD the Jews that the Scriptures "testify of Me" and that Moses "wrote about Me." After He died Jesus appeared to several of His followers, and while walking along a road, He "expounded" to Cleopas and a friend "in all the Scriptures [the Old Testament] the things concerning Himself."[32]

The Old and New Testaments are also both organized the same way. The first half of the Old Testament is history, telling the story of the Jewish people. The second half contains other writings—poetry, Wisdom Literature, and the writings of the prophets. Similarly the first half of the New Testament is history, recording the story of the life of Jesus of Nazareth and the early church. The second half contains letters written to churches and individuals and the book of Revelation.

THE NEW TESTAMENT CONTAINS TWENTY-SEVEN books and letters written by eight or nine writers in the second half of the first century. Each of the first four books tells of the birth, life, ministry, crucifixion, and resurrection of Jesus. They are not exactly biographies of Jesus, but each tells the same story from a different perspective and is written to a different audience. The four are called "gospels," a word that means "good news" or "good story" in Old English.

The first gospel to be written—probably in AD 64 or 65—was traditionally written by John Mark

32 Luke 24:27.
33 1 Peter 5:13.
34 2 Peter 1:16.
35 Matthew 1:22-23, 2:5-6, 17-18; 3:3; 4:14-16, plus others.
36 Paul called him "the beloved physician" (Colossians 4:14).
37 Luke 1:3.
38 John 21:24.

HOC MATHEVS AGENS: HOMINEM
GENERALITER IMPLET:
MARCVS VT ALTA FREMENS:
VOX P DESERTA LEONIS:
IVRA SACERDOCII: LVCAS
TENET ORE IVVENC
MORE VOLANS AQVILÆ:
VERBO PETIT ASTRA IOHANNES:

Tradition connected the writers of the four gospels with the four living creatures in Revelation 1:7, and each writer was given a symbol: Matthew's symbol is an angel (with the "face like a man"), Mark's symbol is a lion, Luke's symbol is an ox or calf, and John's symbol is an eagle. This picture of the four gospel writers and their symbols is from a ninth-century French manuscript in the Bibliotèque Nationale de France.

when he was in Rome with Peter and whom Peter refers to as "Mark my son."[33] Because Mark wrote to Roman readers, he explained Jewish customs more often than the other gospel writers did. Peter was undoubtedly a firsthand source for Mark's gospel and makes a point in his own letter in the New Testament that "we did not follow cunningly devised fables . . . but were eyewitnesses of [Christ's] majesty."[34] Mark's emphasis was on what Jesus *did* more than on what He *said*. Luke (AD 80–85) and Matthew (AD 85–90) wrote their gospels while consulting Mark's gospel as well as other sources including, most scholars assume, an Aramaic document that they call Q. These three—Matthew, Mark, and Luke—are called the Synoptic Gospels because they contain so much of the same information. Many people who had actually seen the events recorded in the gospels were still alive when the three Synoptic Gospels were written.

Matthew, a tax collector, wrote his gospel to Jewish readers and went out of his way to show that Jesus was the fulfillment of Old Testament prophecy.[35] Early church fathers all say that Matthew wrote his gospel in Hebrew and then it was translated into Greek. Luke was a companion of Paul and a medical doctor[36] and is the only Gentile author in the Bible. He presents Christ as the "Son of Man" and writes with particular precision to Gentiles. He says that "it seemed good to me also, having had perfect understanding of all things from the very first, to write to you an orderly account."[37]

The fourth gospel was written by John between AD 90 and 100 and emphasizes the deity of Christ. John makes a point of saying that the "testimony" of the "disciple who . . . wrote" the book "is true"[38] and clearly states that the purpose in writing his gospel is "that you may believe that Jesus is the Christ,

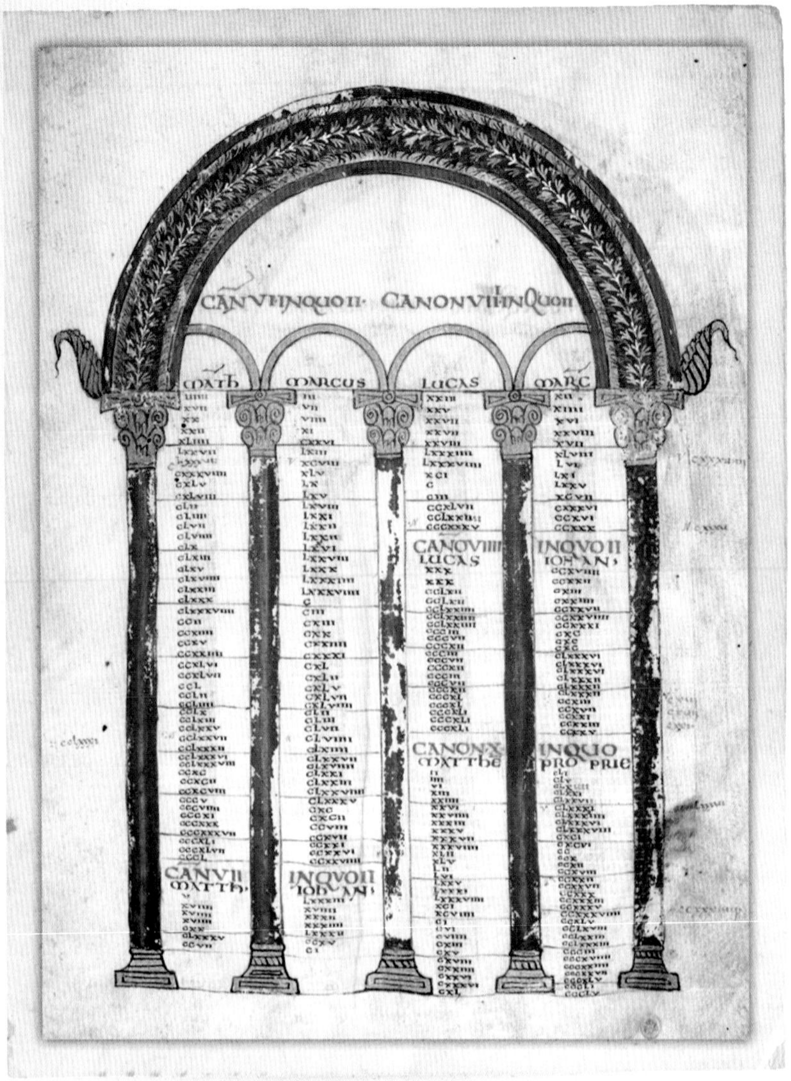

In the fourth century, Eusebius, bishop of Caesarea, divided each of the four gospels into between 232 (John) and 355 (Matthew) numbered sections and then placed the numbers in charts to indicate parallel passages. The usefulness of these charts led them to be included in many medieval Bibles and Gospel Books, including this one, Codex Beneventauns, an eighth-century Italian Gospel Book now in the British Library.

the Son of God, and that believing you may have life in His name."[39] John's gospel does not contain as much narrative as the three synoptic gospels, but focuses on the teachings of Jesus and accounts of His miracles.

Because Matthew, Mark, Luke, and John all tell the same story, numerous "harmonies" of the gospels have been compiled in which the first three or all four gospels are put together in one narrative or compared side by side. The earliest harmony we know about is called the *Diatessaron*, which was the work of Tatian, a pupil of Justyn Martyr, between AD 150 and 160. The *Diatessaron*, compiled in Syriac, is important because it was widely used instead of individual gospels in the Assyrian church for three hundred years. Greek and Old Latin versions of the *Diatessaron* were created a few years later.

A cross-reference system based on a harmony of the gospels that was widely used in the Middle Ages was called the Eusebian Canons. Each of the gospels was divided into small sections[40] by Eusebius, a fourth-century bishop, the sections numbered, and then ten "canon tables" showed parallel passages by listing the numbers side by side.

Acts, the final book of history in the New Testament, was written by Luke shortly after he wrote his gospel and contains the story of the early church as it was directed by the Holy Spirit. Acts tells of the ascension of Christ, the spread of the church, stories of new converts, disagreements among the leaders, the conversion of Paul the apostle, and Paul's imprisonment and transportation to Rome.

The second half of the New Testament contains thirteen letters written by Paul, nine addressed to churches and four to individuals, and the letter to Hebrews, which has traditionally been ascribed to Paul. In addition, there is one letter written by James, probably the brother of Christ; two letters Peter wrote, probably from Rome; and three short letters written by John, traditionally the apostle John. Little is known with certainty of Jude, who wrote the short letter warning Christians of the heresy of Gnosticism, although he may have been the brother of Jesus. The last book is Revelation, the only book in the New Testament that is apocalyptic,

39 John 20:31.
40 This was before the division of the Bible into chapters and verses.
41 Revelation 21:4.
42 Kenyon, *The Story of the Bible*, 28–29.
43 Mark 16:15.

a kind of literature marked by visions, symbolic language, and prophecy. Written by the apostle John just before AD 100 while he was imprisoned on the island of Patmos, Revelation encouraged the faith of Christians in seven cities in modern Turkey. In spite of persecution under the Roman Emperor Domitian, they should be assured of the ultimate, final victory of Jesus Christ, for "God will wipe away every tear from their eyes; there shall be no more death, nor sorrow, nor crying." [41]

In the first century the story of Christ and His teachings were circulated orally and then written down by the gospel writers. Paul and other apostles wrote the letters that became part of Scripture in the middle of the first century, and the Gospel of John and Revelation were written just before AD 100. Then, according to Frederic Kenyon, "we have a period of rather over two hundred years when the various books circulated . . . with no central control to ensure a uniform text. . . . Christianity was . . . exposed to persecutions by the Roman Emperors and governors, when copies of the Scriptures were a special object of search and destruction. . . . [Christians] were thinking only of the substance of the Christian teaching, and caring little for the verbal accuracy of the text." [42]

WHAT IS SO REMARKABLE IS THAT THIS FRAGMENT lets us know that the gospel of John was being read in Egypt . . . within fifty years of John's writing it.

Jews maintained their identity as God's chosen people by preserving their heritage, culture, and traditions. That's why Nehemiah was so upset when he returned from Persia to find that some of the Jews no longer spoke Hebrew. As long as Jews understood Hebrew, there was no need for the Old Testament to be translated. But when they started speaking Greek, Aramaic, and Syriac, the Old Testament was translated into those languages.

Christians, however, were told by Christ to "Go into all the world and preach the gospel to every creature."[43] According to tradition—and with some historical evidence—Thomas took the gospel to India, where the Mar Thoma Church claim him as their founder. Andrew preached in Greece and went as far north as what is modern Ukraine. Peter traveled to Rome where, according to Catholic tradition, he became the city's first bishop. Matthew is said to have gone on several missionary journeys including one to Ethiopia. As they went throughout the world, Christians circulated the gospels and the writings of the apostles and read them in their gatherings, which meant they needed to translate them into other languages, the earliest being Syriac, Latin, and Coptic.

These very early translations are useful to scholars who can compare them with the Hebrew and Greek manuscripts. Other early translations of the Bible were into Ethiopic, Armenian, Georgian, Central Asian, Arabic, Gothic, and Slavonic.

Today more than 5,500 partial or complete Greek New Testament manuscripts have been discovered and preserved. The most complete manuscripts, of course, contain not only the New Testament but the Old Testament as well, with the three oldest and most complete being Vaticanus, Sinaiticus, and Alexandrinus. All three are from the fourth or fifth centuries and contain both testaments or parts of them.

Codex Vaticanus - The oldest nearly complete parchment copy of the Bible discovered to date is Codex Vaticanus, which was in use in the first half of the fourth century. Originally containing the complete Septuagint, except for a portion of the Apocrypha, and most of the New Testament, the codex appeared in 1475 in the first catalog of the Vatican Library, from which it gets its name. Pope Nicholas V founded the library in 1448, and no one knows where the Codex Vaticanus came from, although it is possible the manuscript was brought to Rome by refugees from Constantinople after Muslims captured the city in 1453. It is one of the two most important manuscripts for textual criticism.

Codex Sinaiticus - Found at Egypt's Saint Catherine's monastery in 1844 by Count von Tischendorf, this codex is the oldest complete copy of the New Testament, although only portions of the Septuagint Old Testament still survive because the monks used pages from the manuscript to light their fires in the 1800s. The codex was written about AD 350 by three or four scribes and then heavily annotated by a series of editors between the fourth and twelfth centuries. Originally containing 730 leaves, most of the codex (347 leaves) is at the British Library. (See sidebar on page 35 for the story of its discovery.)

The most complete of the three great manuscripts of the Bible is Codex Alexandrinus, which was copied in the fifth century. It is 10" x 12 1/2" and written in Greek. Codex Alexandrinus was given to the English royal library in 1624 by Cyril Lucar, patriarch of Constantinople, and is now in the British Library. This page contains the end of 2 Peter and the beginning of 1 John.

Codex Alexandrinus - Dating to about AD 425, this beautiful book bound in four volumes is one of the earliest books to use decorations to mark divisions in the text. Although it was copied in the early fifth century, nothing is known about its history until 1621 when Cyril Lucar, who was patriarch of Alexandria, Egypt, took it with him when he moved to Constantinople. In 1627 it was given to King Charles I of England, and it

44 See also page 24.
45 See also page 24.

is now in the British Library. It is interesting to think that Codex Alexandrinus might have been part of the magnificent library in Alexandria, but the library and all its contents were destroyed in a fire in 642.

Some of the other very old and interesting New Testament manuscripts include:

JOHN RYLANDS PAPYRUS (P52) - The oldest existing New Testament fragment discovered so far, it measures 3.5" x 2.5" and contains a few verses from John 18. This papyrus dates from AD 125 to 150. What is so remarkable is that this fragment lets us know that the gospel of John was being read in Egypt—far from Asia Minor where it was written—within fifty years of John's writing it. The John Rylands Papyrus was discovered in Egypt in 1920 and is displayed at the Rylands Library in Manchester, England.

THE CHESTER BEATTY PAPYRI - The New Testament portions of the Chester Beatty Papyri are almost as old as the John Rylands Papyrus, and are far more extensive. Dating to the third century AD, these are portions of three codices. The first contains the four gospels and the book of Acts; the second contains the letters of Paul, including Hebrews; the third contains the book of Revelation. None of these codices is complete. Most of the papyri are at the Chester Beatty Library in Ireland; a few portions are at the University of Michigan.[44]

CODEX EPHRAEMI - This is a palimpsest, a word meaning "scraped again." When parchment became scarce, a scribe might take a manuscript page or an entire codex, wash off the existing words using milk and oat bran, and write on the pages a second time. As time passed, the original writing would begin to

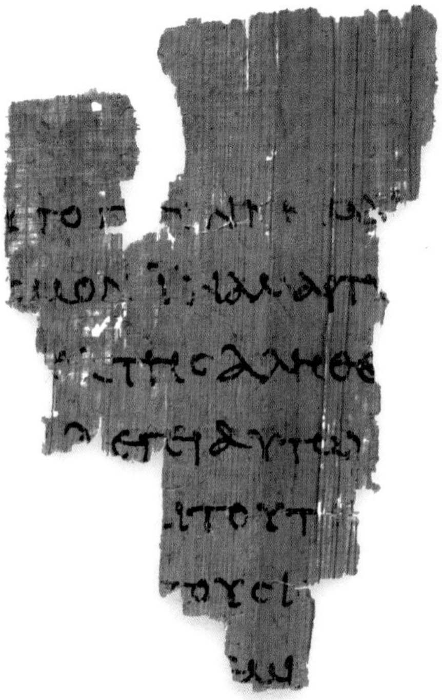

The verso side of the John Rylands Papyrus (P52), shown at left, contains a portion of John 18:37-38. The recto side contains a portion of John 18:31-33. Copied between AD 125 and 150—within only fifty years of John's writing his gospel—this is the oldest existing New Testament fragment discovered so far. The papyrus, shown here in actual size, is on display at the John Rylands University Library in Manchester, England.

appear again, although if the scribe had scraped off the original writing instead of washing it off, the words would be gone forever. Codex Ephraemi was an early fifth-century Greek manuscript of the entire Bible, but in the twelfth century the Bible text was washed off and the sermons of Ephraem the Syrian were written over it. Several renderings of the biblical text have been published, including one by Count von Tischendorf. The codex is in the Bibliotheque Nationale, the National Library in Paris.[45]

CODEX BEZAE - The earliest existing bilingual New Testament manuscript, Codex Bezae is written in Greek on the left side of the page and Latin on the right and may have been written about AD 450. It was discovered in the Saint Ireneaus monastery in Lyons,

The Greek Orthodox Saint Catherine's Monastery is in a small gorge at the foot of Mount Sinai, where Moses received the Ten Commandments. Founded in the sixth century, the monastery was built on the site said to be where Moses saw the burning bush. Saint Catherine's is one of the oldest Christian monasteries in continuous use and contains the world's second largest collection of ancient manuscripts and one of the best collections of early icons.

France, and was donated to Britain's Cambridge University in 1581. Codex Bezae is missing portions of Matthew, John, and Acts, but Codex Claromontanus, which dates from about AD 550 and is in the Bibliotheque Nationale in Paris, contains much of the bilingual text missing from Codex Bezae.

These seven New Testament manuscripts are only the tip of the iceberg of more than 5,500 manuscripts found so far. Codex Siniaticus was discovered in 1844; the discovery of the Chester Beatty Papyri was announced in 1931. The Old Testament Dead Sea Scrolls were found in 1947. What else could possibly be discovered?

In 1892 widowed twin sisters from Cambridge, England, Agnes Smith Lewis and Margaret Dunlop Gibson, received permission to explore the library at Saint Catherine's Monastery. The wealthy, eccentric, and intellectual Mrs. Lewis found the earliest known copy of Old Syriac gospels, dating to the fourth or fifth centuries.

In May 1975, workmen making repairs to Saint Catherine's after a fire discovered a walled-up room in which were seventy boxes with three thousand manuscripts, mostly in Syrian, Slavic, and Coptic. Many were nonbiblical, but there were a few leaves and fragments from Codex Sinaiticus among the find. This makes us wonder what else might be at Saint Catherine's!

In the summer of 2007, a team from the Center for the Study of New Testament Manuscripts in Texas traveled to the National Archive in Tirana, Albania, hoping to photograph thirteen biblical manuscripts, including a sixth-century codex. They found the thirteen manuscripts they expected plus seventeen other manuscripts that were thought to be lost and an additional seventeen manuscripts that were previously entirely unknown to the scholarly community.

The discovery of additional biblical manuscripts will continue, allowing scholars to learn more about the biblical text. "It is reassuring at the end," observed Frederic Kenyon, "to find that the general result of all these discoveries and all this study is to strengthen the proof of the authenticity of the Scriptures, and our conviction that we have in our hands, in substantial integrity, the veritable Word of God." [46]

[46] Kenyon, *The Story of the Bible*, 113.

INDIANA VON TISCHENDORF

A dusty ancient middle-eastern city filled with camels, strange smells, and mysterious traders. A treasure-filled library in an isolated monastery more than two hundred miles to the southeast. Ten days on camelback through the oven-like heat of the desert to a solid wall where acceptable visitors are pulled up in a chair to the entrance thirty feet above ground. A burial vault guarded by the 1,100-year-old skeleton of the monastery janitor. It was at the Saint Catherine's Monastery in the Sinai Desert that Constantin von Tischendorf, a twenty-nine-year-old German biblical scholar with the charm, savvy, and sense of adventure of Indiana Jones, found one of the most important biblical manuscripts ever discovered.

Tischendorf earned his doctorate at Leipzig University at twenty-three, was appointed a lecturer at twenty-five, and at age twenty-seven published a new edition of the Greek New Testament that was acclaimed a masterpiece. At the time, one of the three oldest complete biblical manuscripts was Codex Ephraemi, a fifth-century Bible that had sermons written over the Scripture. The original writing had begun to appear again, but the world's finest scholars had not been able to decipher it. Tischendorf successfully read the biblical text and spent two years copying what he read.

In the spring of 1844, the celebrated Tischendorf took a long and difficult journey to Cairo, visited libraries and monasteries, but did not find any manuscripts of significance. He then traveled ten days on camel to Saint Catherine's, a thirteen-hundred-year-old monastery built on the site of the burning bush where God spoke to Moses at the foot of Mount Sinai. Even today, Saint Catherine's has the second (only to the Vatican) largest collection of ancient manuscripts in the world. After being welcomed by the monks and given a tour, Tischendorf was led to the library. Neglect, ignorance, decay, and dust were everywhere. In the corner in a basket of manuscripts used for kindling to light fires, Tischendorf found 129 parchment leaves of a manuscript of the Septuagint dating from about AD 350. After some shrewd bargaining, Tischendorf was allowed to take forty-three of the 129 leaves with him, which he presented to the library of Leipzig University.

Haunted by the realization that although forty-three leaves of this remarkable manuscript were safely in the Leipzig library, eighty-six leaves were still at Saint Catherine's, Tischendorf made a second trip to Mount Sinai in 1853. Of course the monks remembered the other eighty-six leaves, but they did not know where they were at that time.

Tischendorf prepared for a third trip by getting the endorsement and financing of the Russian czar because he knew the Coptic monks at Saint Catherine's had great respect for the Russian royal family. His 1859 trip went smoothly. He was greeted by the monks who lavished hospitality on him. He was allowed to search the monastery—but found nothing. Before leaving empty-handed Tischendorf was invited to have a drink with a young monk in his cell and presented the monk with a copy of his edition of the Septuagint that had been published in Leipzig. "I also have a copy of the Greek Septuagint," the monk said, and brought out a manuscript wrapped in a red cloth. It was Sinaiticus—not just the eighty-six leaves Tischendorf had seen before, but much more.

All night Tischendorf read one of the oldest existing manuscripts of the Bible. "It really seemed a crime to sleep," he wrote in his diary. The manuscript contained not only portions of the Septuagint Old Testament, but the New Testament as well. It also contained the Epistle of Barnabas (which had been known only in a poor Latin translation) and the Shepherd of Hermas (which was known by title, but no copy was known to exist).

Finding this treasure was only the first step because the monks would not let Tischindorf remove it from the monastery. Eventually he was allowed to copy it in Cairo one quire (eight leaves) at a time. Through convoluted politicking involving the appointment of an archbishop of the Sinai monasteries, the Russian ambassador to Turkey persuaded the monks at Saint Catherine's to "lend" the manuscript to the Russian czar, and Tischendorf personally carried Codex Sinaiticus to Saint Petersburg.

In 1933 the Soviet Union, needing hard currency, sold the manuscript to Great Britain for 100,000 pounds. Today 347 leaves of Codex Sinaiticus are on display at the British Library in London. The forty-three leaves that Tischendorf took from Saint Catherine's in 1844 are still at Leipzig University in Germany. Fragments of six leaves are at the National Library of Russia in Saint Petersburg, and twelve additional leaves and forty fragments are at Saint Catherine's, discovered by workmen repairing the monastery in 1975.

4

THE EARLY YEARS OF THE CHURCH

(Right) In 846, four hundred years after translating the Bible into Latin, Jerome was made the subject of an introductory page in a lavishly illuminated Bible presented to Charles the Bald. The top panel shows Jerome sailing from Rome to Bethleham and being paid for his work. The middle panel shows him translating the Bible and explaining it to his followers, with those at the right making copies. The bottom panel shows Jerome distributing the Latin Vulgate Bible to monks who take copies to churches. The Vivian Bible is in the Bibliotèque Nationale de France.

SOME DISPUTES IN THE EARLY CHURCH WERE PERSONAL, some were theological, and some were political—just like church disputes today.

Even while Jesus was alive, His followers started positioning themselves to be seen as the most important. James and John, who were brothers, audaciously asked to sit on either side of Christ "in Your glory."[47] And it was not long before the Christians divided into factions—some saying they followed Paul, some saying they followed Apollos, and others saying they followed Peter. Paul himself was amazed that shortly after becoming Christians, the believers in Galatia began following "a different gospel."[48]

So which factions of Christianity were the true ones? Was it the teaching of Paul, of Apollos, or of Peter? It is easy for us today to say that the guideline for discerning truth from heresy should be Scripture, but what was Scripture? And who interpreted it? The first question will be answered in this chapter; the second will be discussed in chapter 6. In addition to needing to know which books and letters were part of the New Testament in order to give guidance in discerning heresy from truth, Christians needed to know what was Scripture to know which writings to hide in times of persecution.

The early church faced many Gnostic teachers who taught that salvation comes through having special knowledge of the secrets of the universe and that material things are evil and spiritual things are good.

47 Mark 10:37.
48 Galatians 1:6.

HIERONIMVS ROMA CONDISCERE VERBA
THRONO FVLTVS VBIQVE DO

The early church also heard Arius say that Jesus was not fully divine but was a created being, and it heard Pelagius say that a person's will can choose good over evil without God's help. Marcion said that the God of the Old Testament was not as good as the God of love and grace in the New Testament. Montanus told his followers that Christ was about to come back to set up His kingdom and, of course, give special privileges to Montanists, disciples of Montanus. The church had to decide whether these ideas accurately reflected Christian teaching. (All of these were declared to be heresy, by the way.) To decide which teachings did not square with Scripture, the church first had to know which writings were part of Scripture.

"The historic Christian belief is that the Holy Spirit, who controlled the writing of the individual books, also controlled their selection and collection,"[49] said biblical scholar F.F. Bruce. But that does not tell us how the twenty-seven books of the New Testament were identified. One criterion was that a book had to be written by one of the twelve apostles or Paul, or, in the case of Mark and Luke, with apostolic approval. But to give themselves credibility and authority, some writers said that what they had written had come from the pen of an apostle, even though it had not.

THE OLD TESTAMENT CANON HAD BEEN EFFECTIVELY established before the time of Christ.[50] It had been translated into Greek in the third century BC, and Jesus and the New Testament writers quoted from thirty-four of the thirty-nine books of the Old Testament. At the end of the first century, when Rabbi Johanan and others were concerned about the loss of Jewish identity and heritage because of the destruction of Jerusalem

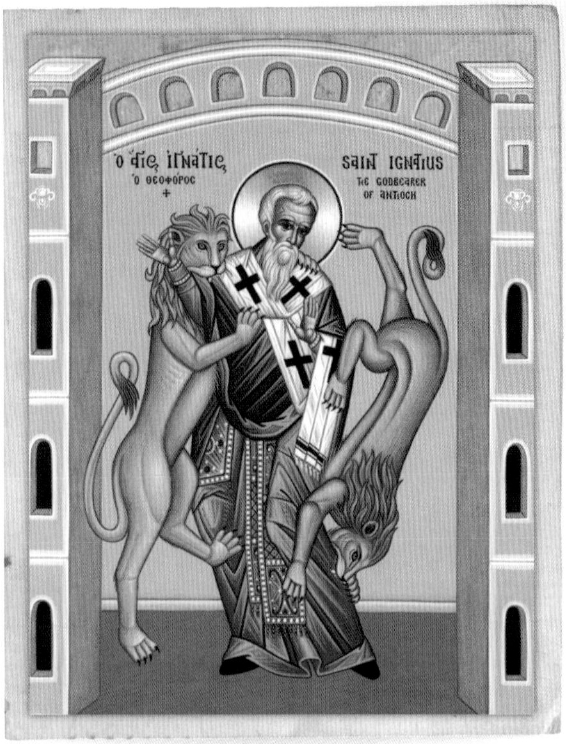

Ignatius was made bishop of Antioch about AD 69. Forty years later the Emperor Trajan sentenced Ignatius to death and brought him to Rome. In a letter to the church at Rome, Ignatius said, "Suffer me to be food of wild beasts." When he got to Rome, he was taken to the Coliseum where he was devoured by lions. This icon celebrates his martyrdom.

and the influence of Christian teaching in synagogues, the Council of Jamnia preserved the use of Hebrew by rejecting the Septuagint (which was increasingly used by Christians) and separating Christians from Jewish communities. The Council also confirmed that the Old Testament canon consisted of the thirty-nine books we now have. But at the end of the first century there was not yet an accepted New Testament canon.

As Christianity spread, converts wanted to know the story and teachings of Jesus and the apostles, and they read in their worship services the accounts that had been written down. In the second century, Justin Martyr described the worship service of Christians on the Lord's Day as reading the "memoirs of the apostles [the New Testament] or the writings of the Prophets [the Old Testament]" followed by a sermon, prayers, the Eucharist, and a collection to help the or-

49 F. F. Bruce, *The New Testament Documents: Are They Reliable?* (Grand Rapids: William B. Eerdmans Publishing Co., 1981), 16.
50 See pages 22-23.
51 Willy Rordorf, "The Bible in the Teaching and the Liturgy of Early Christian Communities," in *The Bible in Greek Christian Antiquity*, ed. and trans. by Paul M. Blowers (Notre Dame, Indiana: University of Notre Dame Press, 1997), 69.
52 2 Peter 3:15-16.
53 Bruce, *The New Testament Documents: Are They Reliable?* 17.

(Above left) In the middle of the second century, Christians were persecuted and killed. If only the aged and gentle Polycarp would say that Caesar was lord and reproach Christ, his life could be spared. Polycarp refused to "blaspheme my King who saved me." It is said that the fires did not burn him and so the executioner pierced his body with a sword. The illustration is from Foxe's Book of Martyrs.

(Above) Hippolytus was a Roman soldier who, at the direction of Emperor Valerian in AD 258, helped to torture and execute St. Lawrence. As the result of St. Lawrence's example, Hippolytus became a Christian and was then himself sentenced by Valerian to be torn apart by horses. The painting is by the Dutch painter Dieric Bouts (1415-1475).

phans and widows and those in need. Very few written records of early Christian sermons and prayers have survived, but by the second century accounts of the life and teachings of Jesus and the apostles were quoted as Scripture, just as the Old Testament was.

Spurious writings claiming to have been penned by the apostles were widespread, including the Secret Book of James, the Gospel of Thomas, and the Apocalypse of Paul. As many as fifty gospels were in circulation, not just the four in the Bible. Determining the New Testament canon was as much a matter of omitting spurious writings as it was selecting writings inspired by the Holy Spirit. The "New Testament represents only a very limited selection among the . . . Sayings, Acts, Epistles, and Apocalypses which were circulating at the time of the primitive Church." [51]

The four gospels were all written in the first century, and because of their apostolic authorship or authority they were circulated together. About 180, Bishop Irenaeus said that just as there are "four quarters of the world in which we live," the Church should have "four pillars" of the gospels. The Acts of the Apostles had authority because it was written by Luke, a companion of Paul who wrote what was "delivered" to him by "eyewitnesses" so that he "had perfect understanding of all things." The letters of Paul and the letter to the Hebrews, which is frequently attributed to Paul, were also accepted as part of Scripture without much question. In fact, Peter equates the letters of Paul with "the rest of the Scriptures."[52] Only a few books that are now at the end of the New Testament appear to have been in question by the end of the second century.

The earliest known list of New Testament books was drawn up about 140 by Marcion, a heretic who believed that the church should separate itself from the Old Testament and its influences, including books written by the apostles that "seemed to him to be infected with Judaism."[53] His list of books that constituted the New Testament canon included parts of the gospel of Luke and Acts and ten of the letters

Constantine the Great was Roman emperor from AD 306 until his death in 337. Unlike his predecessor Diocletian, who vigorously persecuted Christians and destroyed their Scriptures and places of worship, Constantine converted to Christianity and effectively made it the state religion. He moved the capital of the empire from Rome to Constantinople, a city he built and consecrated in 330. This mosaic in Hagia Sofia in Constantinople shows Constantine presenting the city as a tribute to Mary and the Christ Child.

of Paul that he thought supported his own heretical ideas. Another list, the Muratorian Canon, which is closer to our twenty-seven New Testament books, dates from the end of the second century, although we do not know who wrote it.

In the third century Origen—and a few years later Eusebius—said some people questioned the canonicity of Hebrews, 2 Peter, 2 and 3 John, James, and Jude. In 367 Athanasius identified the twenty-seven books of our New Testament as alone being canonical. When the Synod of Hippo (in 393) and the Synod of Carthage (in 397) identified the books of the New Testament as we now know them, they were merely confirming what the church had already determined were New Testament books through their use in teaching and worship.

F.F. Bruce says, "One thing must be emphatically stated. The New Testament books did not become authoritative for the Church because they were formally included in a canonical list; on the contrary, the Church included them in her canon because she already regarded them as divinely inspired, recognizing their innate worth and generally apostolic authority, direct or indirect." What the synods at Hippo and Carthage did, says Bruce, "was not to impose something new upon the Christian communities but to codify what was already the general practice of those communities."[54]

THE PERSECUTION OF THE CHURCH WAS THE SECOND reason Christians needed to know which books were in the New Testament canon. Manuscripts were precious because they had to be hand written. When the Roman police demanded that a Christian hand over a book so that it could be burned, that person would be more likely to hide a manuscript containing Scripture and turn over a document that was not part of the canon.

For 250 years the early Christians were horribly persecuted by the Roman authorities—not so much for religious reasons as for political ones. The Romans tended to be tolerant of religions and incorporated local gods of conquered areas into the Roman pantheon. But Christianity was different. Christians did not give their primary allegiance to the Roman emperor, and so Rome viewed Christianity as a threat to its society, a society that was disintegrating anyway.

The first major persecution of Christians was under the Emperor Nero in AD 64, who may himself have been the one to start a disastrous nine-day fire in Rome. To deflect blame from himself,

54 Ibid., 22.

Nero said the fire was caused by Christians. Then, according to *Foxe's Book of Martyrs*, he sewed some Christians in wild animals skins so they would be torn to pieces by dogs, crucified others, and some he made into torches and set on fire. The persecution under Nero was the first of ten major persecutions. The tenth, under Diocletian in 303, ordered that Christian books and churches be burned, Christian congregations be dissolved, and the property of Christians be confiscated. As tensions mounted, Diocletian ordered that Christians who refused to worship Roman gods should be subjected to torture.

The stories of Christians who chose to die or be tortured instead of denying their faith are inspiring. In the middle of the second century, a bloodthirsty crowd demanded the death of Polycarp, an eighty-six-year-old bishop who, as a young man, was said to have known the apostle John. Polycarp was offered freedom from torture if he denied Christ. "For eighty and six years have I been his servant, and he has done me no wrong; how then can I blaspheme my King who saved me?" he replied. The scholar Tertullian became a Christian when he saw the courage of Christian martyrs and said, "The blood of the martyrs is the seed of the church."

Succession of political power in the Roman Empire was not orderly. Diocletian died in December 311. In 312 Constantine and Maxentius, two contenders for Diocletian's position as emperor, met in battle nine miles north of Rome. According to Eusebius, on the afternoon before the fight Constantine saw a flaming cross in the sky with the words in Greek, "In this sign conquer." Early the next morning he heard a voice commanding him to have his soldiers mark their shields with a symbol of Christ. Constantine won the

When a dispute arose about the teachings of Arius, who said that Christ was not fully divine, the Emperor Constantine invited Christian bishops to a council in Nicaea. About three hundred of them arrived at a consensus that Arius was not correct and wrote a creed to be used by the entire church. The council also set a date for Easter, which had been celebrated at different times around the empire. This picture is a mid-eighteenth-century Russian icon.

Jerome's translation of the Bible into Latin, called the Vulgate, was used by the Roman Catholic Church for more than fifteen hundred years. In addition, this scholar, exegete, and librarian wrote many commentaries on Scripture. This painting by fifteenth-century Italian Niccolo Antonio Colantonio shows Jerome in his study in Bethlehem and illustrates a medieval legend. Jerome was said to have removed a thorn from the paw of a lion, who then became his constant and gentle companion.

battle, and with his brother-in-law Licinius he became the unchallenged ruler of the empire. It was one of the great turning points in history because Christians were no longer persecuted for their faith. Instead they were heralds of the new official faith of the Roman Empire.

"Was his conversion sincere . . . or a consummate stroke of political wisdom?" asks historian Will Durant. "Probably the latter." But whether Constantine's conversion was motivated by his faith or his politics, the effect was significant. In the following ten years Constantine's actions became more pro-Christian. He "gave money to needy congregations, built several churches, . . . and forbade the worship of images in" Constantinople, the city he founded in modern Turkey to become the new capital of the Roman Empire. "He gave his sons an orthodox Christian education, and financed his mother's Christian philanthropies. The Church rejoiced in blessings beyond any expectation."[55] The move of the empire's capital from Rome to Constantinople, where Europe and Asia meet, marked the beginning of the split between the Roman and Orthodox churches. British journalist Malcolm Muggeridge makes the distinction that Christ gave Christianity to the world (a faith); and Constantine gave Christendom to the world (a politic).[56]

In spite of more than two hundred years of persecution, the Christian church had grown and developed an organization. A bishop was in charge of a group of churches, and as early as the end of the first century, Clement, bishop of Rome, wrote to Christians in Corinth with the assumption that he had authority over other bishops. When Constantine made Christianity an approved religion, and then, in effect,

55 Will Durant, *Caesar and Christ*, vol. 3 of *The Story of Civilization*, (New York: Simon and Schuster, 1944, 1972), 655, 657.
56 Malcolm Muggeridge, *The End of Christendom* (Grand Rapids: William B. Eerdmans Publishing Co., 1980).
57 The Council of Nicaea made no statements on what constituted the canon of Scripture.
58 This was the same council that decided that the deuterocanonical books (the Apocrypha) were part of Scripture.

the state religion, the church's political organization flourished and the bishop of Rome solidified his position of leadership.

A dispute arose about the teachings of Arius, who said that Christ was not fully divine. To settle the matter and several other questions, Constantine in 325 invited the bishops of the church to meet at Nicaea, less than fifty miles from Constantinople. More than three hundred bishops overwhelmingly declared Arianism to be heretical and wrote a creed that was to be used by the entire church—an early version of what we now know as the Nicene Creed. This was the first council of the entire church since the Jerusalem Council described in Acts 15, and its significance cannot be overestimated.[57] It marked the end of a pagan empire and the prelude to the Middle Ages when Christianity would dominate Europe.

> CHRISTIANS WERE SEVERELY PERSECUTED . . . , then tolerated, and then became bearers of the official religion of the empire. The blood of the martyrs became the seed of the church as the message of Christ was taken throughout the empire and beyond.

One of the more interesting acts of Constantine was his writing to Eusebius that because many people were becoming Christians in Constantinople, there would be more churches and that Eusebius should "order fifty copies of the sacred Scriptures, the provision and use of which you know to be most needful for the instruction of the Church." The manuscripts were to be written "on well-prepared parchment by copyists most skillful in the art of accurate and beautiful writing, which must be very legible and easily portable in order that they may be used." The task Eusebius was given was not just to print another fifty copies of the Bible. Each one had to be handwritten. It is tempting to think that Codex Vaticanus and Codex Sinaiticus were two of the fifty copies that were created for the churches in Constantinople. Their dates would make that possible, but there is no other evidence. What is significant is that Constantine assumed Eusebius knew what was meant by "the sacred Scriptures." Constantine's letter was written nearly a century before church councils confirmed what Eusebius and the church already knew—which writings constituted Scripture.

THE MOST IMPORTANT AND INFLUENTIAL TRANSLATION of Scripture ever made was the Septuagint translation of the Old Testament into Greek. A close second, though, was the translation of the entire Bible into Latin in the early fifth century, a translation called "the Vulgate," meaning "the language of the people," or "popular version." It was the official translation used by the Roman Church for more than fifteen hundred years and influenced art, culture, and church life during the Middle Ages and for years afterwards. In 1546 the Council of Trent[58] declared the Vulgate to be the only authentic Latin text of the Bible, even though by that time Latin was obsolete as an everyday spoken language.

The Old Testament and the twenty-seven New Testament books had been circulating among the churches in Greek, in Latin, and in other languages.

Eusebius, Bishop of Caesarea, was the "Father of Church History," a theologian, and creator of the "canon tables" that identified the passages in the four different gospels that recorded the same events. His history of the first three centuries of the church included the famous account of the conversion of Constantine, who later told Eusebius to order fifty copies of the Bible for the churches in Constantinople.

The various Latin manuscripts differed in style and quality of translation, and, as they were copied, textual variations crept in. There was a need for an accurate Latin translation of the Bible. In 382 Pope Damasus asked his secretary, Jerome, a scholar and linguist, to make a revision of the various Old Latin translations of the four gospels. Jerome worked energetically for two years, and when Damasus died in 384, moved to Bethlehem, where the project grew to include the entire Bible. While Jerome made use of the Septuagint, he eventually translated all thirty-nine Old Testament books from Hebrew, not Greek. Jerome did not include the Apocrypha in his translation of the Bible, making it clear in his prologues that these books, while edifying, were not canonical. The Apocrypha was included in later Vulgate manuscripts, but the Latin translation was not Jerome's.

The Vulgate is a composite work with a complex history. Years of copying brought in many variations, and in about 800 Alcuin, an English scholar and theologian working at the direction of Charlemagne, emperor of the Holy Roman Empire, produced a revised text.

Some early partial manuscripts exist, but the earliest complete Vulgate Bible is Codex Amiatinus, an eighth-century copy of a sixth-century manuscript. Missionaries to England from North Africa founded a number of monasteries, and two in the northeast of England made three massive Bibles, one for each monastery and one as a gift for the pope. Only the pope's Bible survives—Codex Amiatinus. Its 2,060 pages are each 13-1/4" x 19-1/2", it weighs about seventy-five pounds, and is today in Florence, Italy.[59]

WHAT A DIFFERENCE FIVE HUNDRED YEARS MAKES! When the New Testament was written in the first century, Christianity was considered to be a sect of Judaism. Over the next four hundred years, Christians were severely persecuted by the powerful Roman Empire, then tolerated, and then became bearers of the official religion of the empire. The blood of the martyrs became the seed of the church as the message of Christ was taken throughout the empire and beyond. Being a part of the power structure of the empire gave the church—Orthodox in the east and Roman in the west—opportunities to preach the gospel, make converts, study the Scriptures, build centers of worship, and over the years become corrupted by politics, power, and wealth.

The story of Christ's birth, ministry, death, and resurrection was circulated very early in four gospels, which, along with the story of the early church in Acts and the writings of Paul and other apostles, were confirmed to be Scripture. The Bible was translated into Syriac, Coptic, and more than half a dozen other languages. The most important early translation was the Vulgate, a Latin translation begun by Jerome in the late fourth century, and the official Bible of the Roman church for more than fifteen hundred years.

59 Neil R. Lightfoot, *How We Got the Bible*, 3rd ed., (Grand Rapids: Baker Books, 2003), 79.

Nag Hammadi Codex II, opened at the conclusion of the Gospel of Thomas, is one of the codices found in Upper Egypt in 1945.

GNOSTICISM, NAG HAMMADI, AND *THE DA VINCI CODE*

Most people consider ancient heresies obscure, boring, and irrelevant, even though the teachings of Arius show up in Jehovah's Witness and Unitarian theology, and certain teachings of the Gnostics show up in the doctrines of Mormonism. But in the twenty-first century, one of the primary heresies facing the early church, Gnosticism, is alive, well, and making news.

Among the dozens of deviations from Orthodox Christianity that seduced early Christians, the most influential was Gnosticism, which was not so much an organized religious system as a wide variety of beliefs in which the material world was thought to be by nature evil and salvation was said to come through a higher or spiritual knowledge of the mysteries of the universe. Stephan Hoeller, a modern Gnostic, explains that Gnosticim is a "conviction that direct, personal and absolute knowledge of the authentic truths of existence is accessible to human beings . . . and that the attainment of such knowledge must always constitute the supreme achievement of human life."[60] In pre-Christian times Gnosticism's mystical thought influenced some Jewish thinkers and later it also had an influence on some early Christians. "Gnosticism . . . was not a heresy so much as a rival" to Christianity.[61]

Various Gnostic influences on Christian beliefs were condemned as heresies by early church councils and the church fathers. In his *Against Heresies*, Irenaeus summarized the Gnostic teachings before pointing out why they were wrong, and until the mid-nineteenth century Irenaeus's description of Gnosticism was the best available. Various Gnostic groups had mostly disappeared by the fifth century and would be nothing more than an interesting footnote for students of early church history if not for three recent events.

First, in 1945 a library of more than fifty Gnostic texts was found at Nag Hammadi, Egypt, about forty miles northwest of Luxor and the Valley of the Kings. The best known of these texts is the Gospel of Thomas, which is not an account of the life of Christ, but 114 sayings attributed to Jesus. Other texts (popularly known as *The Gnostic Gospels*) include the Gospel of Mary, the Secret Book of James, the Gospel of Truth, and the Acts of Peter. None of these is canonical, but they created quite a stir when they were discovered. Headlines promised a new look at the life of Christ, playing on popular intrigue with anything new, secret, or suppressed—a clever marketing twist on the early church's condemnation of Gnosticism.

Second, in 2003 *The Da Vinci Code*, one of the bestselling books of all times, suggested that the Gnostic Gospels had as much—or more—validity as the New Testament books and that their exclusion from the canon occurred at the time of Constantine (a misinterpretation of Constantine's request to Eusebius to make fifty copies of Scripture for the churches in Constantinople). *The Da Vinci Code* was a well-written novel with suspense, intrigue, and murder, but because it suggested that what the church has taught about Jesus is wrong and that Jesus and Mary Magdalene were married, it heightened interest in Gnostic writings.

Third, in May 2006 *The National Geographic* published a lead article on the discovery of a Coptic manuscript of The Gospel of Judas, which contains "the secret account of the revelation that Jesus spoke" with Judas Iscariot. The magazine gave the article major promotion and presented Judas not as the disciple who betrayed Jesus, but as the disciple who was the closest to Him and turned Him over to the authorities because Jesus had asked him to do so. *The New York Times* quoted an executive of the geographic society that The Gospel of Judas "is considered by scholars and scientists to be the most significant ancient, nonbiblical text to be found in the past 60 years"[62]—a claim that is more hype than fact.

In spite of the headlines and press releases, there is nothing new about the Gnostic texts. The Gospel of Judas has been known for centuries. Irenaeus called it "fictitious history." The fourth-century historian and theologian Eusebius distinguished "between those writings which, according to the tradition of the Church, are true and genuine and recognized" and "those which the heretics put forward under the name of the apostles; including, for instance, such books as the Gospels of Peter, of Thomas, of Matthias, . . . and the Acts of Andrew and John and the other apostles." (The Gospel of Thomas was among the manuscripts at Nag Hammadi.) The "thought and purport of their contents are completely out of harmony with true orthodoxy and clearly show themselves that they are the forgeries of heretics . . . to be cast aside as altogether absurd and impious."[63]

In spite of the warnings of Irenaeus and Eusebius, Gnosticism is alive and well.

60 Stephan Hoeller, *The Gnostic Jung and the Seven Sermons to the Dead*, (Wheaton, Illinois: Theosophical Publishing House, 1989), 11.
61 Durant, *Caesar and Christ*, 604.
62 John Noble Wilford and Laurie Goodstein, "'Gospel of Judas' Surfaces after 1,700 Years," *New York Times*, April 6, 2006.
63 http://www.ntcanon.org/Eusebius.shtml (accessed August 27, 2009).

5

THE MIDDLE AGES

(Right) The first page of Matthew in the Capuchin's Bible (1170-1180) starts with the Latin Vulgate "Liber generationis Iesu Chri filii David" ("The book of the geneology of Jesus Christ, the Son of David"). The "iber" of "Liber" is in the lower right portion of the "L," which is filled with a Tree of Jesse. Frequently used in medieval art—a stained glass Tree of Jesse window in Chartres Cathedral also dates from the twelfth century—the Tree of Jesse pictures the genealogy of Christ as a descendent of David, son of Jesse (see Isaiah 11:1). Christ appears at the center top with Mary beneath Him. King David is at the center bottom, coming out of the side of Jesse, who is reclining along the bottom of the "L." The Capuchin's Bible, which is 13" x 17-3/4", is in the Bibliotèque Nationale de France.

UNLESS YOU HAVE ENCOUNTERED A RENAISSANCE FESTIVAL with its twenty-first century depiction of minstrels and maidens, jousting and juggling, feasting and merrymaking, you probably know little about the Middle Ages, the thousand years between the fall of the Roman Empire and the Reformation.

This was the time of Robin Hood, of Joan of Arc, of the code of chivalry, and of King Arthur and the Knights of the Round Table. During the Middle Ages the church in the East faced the new challenge of Islam, a challenge the church in the West took up with enthusiasm in the Crusades. During the Middle Ages the Roman Church in the West touched everyone's life, from the richest king to the poorest serf. Almost everyone belonged to the church, was baptized in the church, would pray in the church, marry in the church, hear sermons in the church, live by the church's laws, and pay taxes to support the church. The parish church was the center of town, the cathedral was the center of a city with a bishop, and kings paid honor to the pope. The Roman Church became the primary political and cultural power of the time.

With the church dominating all of life, it is no wonder that the stories and teachings of the Bible permeated people's thoughts and lives to an extent that is difficult for us to comprehend today. Its message was told in drama, art, poetry, and architecture. And some of the most spectacular relics of the Middle Ages are beautiful

GENERATIONIS .I.
ihu xpi filij dauid. filij abraham. A M.I.
braham genuit ysaac. Ysaac autem L.xiiii.
genuit iacob. Iacob autem genuit iu I.I.
dam et fratres eius. Iudas autem ge viii
nuit phares et zaram de thamar. Pha 7.v.
res autem genuit esrom. esrom autem iii
genuit aram. Aram autem genuit ami
nadab. aminadab autem genuit na
ason. Naason autem genuit salmon.
salmon autem genuit booz de rachab.
Booz autem genuit obed ex ruth. obed
autem genuit iesse. Iesse autem genu
it dauid regem. Dauid autem rex genu
it salomonem ex ea que fuit urie. Sa
lomon autem genuit roboam. roboa
autem genuit abiam. Abia autem
genuit asa. asa autem genuit iosa
phat. Iosaphat autem genuit ioram.
ioram autem genuit oziam. Ozias au
tem genuit ioatham. ioatham autē
genuit achaz. Achaz autem genuit
ezechiam. ezechias autem genuit ma
nassen. Manasses autem genuit amon.
amon autem genuit iosiam. Iosias
autem genuit iechoniam et fratres
eius in transmigratione babylonis.
Et post transmigratione babylonis.
iechonias genuit salathiel. Salathiel
autem genuit zorobabel. zorobabel
autem genuit abiud. Abiud autem

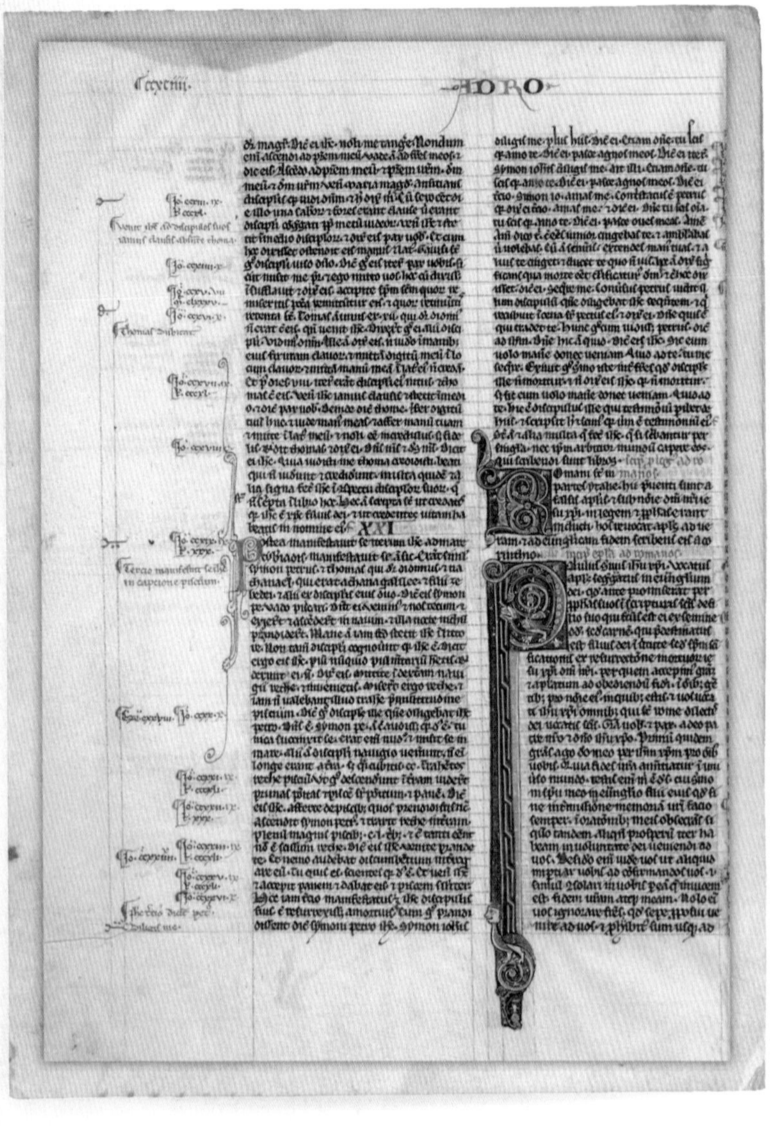

Between the twelfth and thirteenth centuries, Bibles became smaller, were produced in single volumes, had supplementary material added, and the text was divided into chapters. These changes tended to originate in Paris, leading to the term "Paris Bible." This page contains the end of John (chapter number "21" is in the left column in blue and red) followed by the beginning of Romans. The Bible contains subject headings in the margins, cross references, a running title (This page has "AD RO"; the facing page has "MANOS"—"To Romans."), and page numbers ("CCXCIIII" is 294). This 1236 Paris Bible, which is 8" x 12-3/8," is in the Bibliotèque Nationale de France.

illuminated manuscripts in which the text of the Bible is surrounded by sumptuous illustrations, elaborate ornamental decoration, and encased in costly bindings.

The Bible's story during the Middle Ages begins with its translation into Gothic in the fourth century and ends with its translation into English in the fourteenth. Both translators were declared heretics by the Roman Church—the first for saying Christ was not fully divine, the second for teaching that authority rests with Scripture and not with the Church and pope.

His name meant "Little Wolf" and his family had been captured by the Goths when they plundered Asia Minor. Born in 311, Wulfila (or Ulfilas) learned several languages, became an official in the Gothic court, and was sent to Constantinople as part of a diplomatic mission to the Emperor Constantine. He became a bishop there at twenty-nine and then moved to what is now Bulgaria.

In 350 Wulfila decided to translate the Bible into Gothic, an unwritten language containing words for only concrete ideas. He first had to invent an alphabet, which he adapted from Greek, but the real challenge was to invent words to communicate the abstract concepts of the Bible. Wulfila's translation included all the books of the Bible except Kings, which contains stories of battles and military conquests. The Gothic tribes were "fond of war, and were in more need of restraints to check their military passions than of spurs to urge them on to deeds of war," said the historian Philostorgius.

Single-handedly Wulfila created the first Germanic written language. But, like most Goths, he was an Arian and he believed that Christ was a created being and therefore not fully God.

64 Christopher de Hamel, *The Book: A History of The Bible*, (New York: Phaidon Press, 2001), 56.

THE GOTHS, ALONG WITH THE HUNS AND GERmanic tribes from the north, were the "barbarians" who were responsible for the eventual downfall of the Roman Empire, which brought on the Middle Ages. When Constantine moved his throne to Constantinople (in modern Turkey) in 330, the bishop of Rome—the pope—filled the power vacuum left by the departure of the emperor and began the church's domination of Europe. Then the church divided into the Catholic Church in Rome and the Orthodox Church in Constantinople. Tensions between the East and West grew until 1054 when the split became hostile because of differences in doctrine, language, politics, and geography, and each side excommunicated representatives of the other.

ONE OTHER DIFFERENCE BETWEEN THE TWO branches of the Christian church was the Bible they used. While the Latin Vulgate was the Bible of the West, the East read the Bible in Greek. Most surviving Greek manuscripts are not the entire Bible but consist of one or several books, most commonly the four gospels or the Psalms. One of the earliest eastern Greek manuscripts is a fifth-century copy of Genesis that had more than three hundred miniature illustrations. The Cotton Genesis—so called because it was part of a library put together in the seventeenth century by Sir Robert Bruce Cotton in London—survived for 1,250 years, but a fire in 1731 left only charred remains of eighteen out of what was originally more than four hundred handwritten and illustrated pages.

In 726 Leo III, emperor of the Eastern Empire, issued an edict against the use of images because of the second commandment's prohibition of idol worship. He ordered the destruction of religious art, including icons, and for more than one hundred years Bibles or Scripture portions created in the East did not have any illustrations.

Medieval churches and monasteries were filled with paintings, mosaics, and sculptures depicting biblical characters. Among the most spectacular are the mosaics of St. Mark's Basilica in Venice. The building was consecrated in 1094. In the twelfth century mosaics were added depicting events of the New Testament. The mosaics added in the thirteenth century show events from Genesis and Exodus and other Old Testament books. Interwoven are scenes from various saints, especially Mark, whose body was in the basilica from 828 until 1968.

Once this prohibition was lifted, however, Gospel Books became elaborately illustrated. Studios Monastery in Constantinople, one of the most important centers of manuscript creation, established rules such as, "A scribe whose attention wandered during the task of copying could be punished by a diet of bread and water; a scribe who did not keep his parchment clean could be subjected to 130 penances; a scribe who broke his pen in a fit of temper could be subjected to 30 penances."[64]

"If there is one theme which runs right through the history of Greek Bibles" from the East,

Legend says that in the early thirteenth century in a Benedictine monastery east of Prague, the monk Hermannus was sentenced to be buried alive for breaking his monastic vows. He agreed to make the most magnificent book the world had ever seen, but he had to do it in one night. When he realized he would not be able to finish his task, he asked the devil to help him and included in the Bible a fanciful image of the devil. Codex Gigas, *the so-called Devil's Bible and the largest medieval Bible in the world, is at the National Library of Sweden.*

says historian and librarian Christopher de Hamel, "it is that the books were made to be used. They were seldom luxury manuscripts simply for the delight of private owners."[65] In the eleventh century a wealthy landowner left portions of the Bible in his will and stated that they "must be used, as it is necessary, when it is necessary, and where it is necessary."[66] In the West illuminated manuscripts were created more for their beauty. The designs were sometimes so elaborate that the words were hardly readable.

DURING THE MIDDLE AGES MUHAMMAD, VIEWED by his followers as the last and greatest of the prophets, founded Islam. Six years after Muhammad's death in 632, his followers conquered Palestine, took control of Jerusalem, and built the Dome of the Rock. This shrine covers the rock where, Muslims believe, Muhammad ascended to heaven after a miraculous night journey from Mecca accompanied by the archangel Gabriel. It is the same rock where, Jews believe, Abraham built an altar to sacrifice his son Isaac.

Muslims swept across North Africa and entered Europe at Spain in the middle of the eighth century. They built a civilization that reached the peak of its glory in tenth-century Cordova, a city of half a million people with mosques, palaces, and libraries, including one with a reported 500,000 manuscripts. At this time Islamic philosophy, science, and technology were all more advanced than that in Western Europe, which was in the middle of the Dark Ages. The Islamic control of Palestine eventually led the Roman Church to launch the Crusades to recapture Jerusalem and the Holy Land from the "infidels." Pope Urban II said that any Christian who died in the first crusade, which began in 1095, would receive immediate forgiveness for his sins. The crusades lasted nearly two hundred years, and the purpose expanded to include campaigns against other unbelievers and political enemies of the popes.

THE MIDDLE AGES CAN BE DIVIDED INTO THE Dark Ages, which lasted until about 1000; the High Middle Ages, from 1000 to 1300; and the Late Middle Ages until about 1492, when Columbus discovered the New World. The Dark Ages was marked by "confusion, ignorance, and disorder. Classical culture was abandoned, and libraries, buildings, and works of art were either destroyed or neglected. . . . The one institution left standing was the Church."[67] It was only natural, therefore, that "the Bible was at the center of medieval religious thought; it was the supreme textbook of the medieval world, essential for understanding its attitudes, its beliefs, its enthusiasms, its culture, and its art."[68]

Everyone knew about the Bible, but most could not hear it read in their own language because

65 Ibid., 63.
66 Ibid., 63.
67 H. S. Miller, *General Biblical Introduction: From God to Us* (Houghton, New York: Word-Bearer Press, 1960), 324.
68 Rosalind Brooke and Christopher Brooke, *Popular Religion in the Middle Ages: Western Europe, 1000-1300* (London: Thames and Hudson, 1984), 130.
69 Quoted in Paul Cavill, ed. *The Christian Tradition in Anglo-Saxon England: Approaches to Current Scholarship and Teaching* (Cambridge: D.S. Brewer, 2004), 103.

Magnificent medieval cathedrals such as Salisbury (left) in England (consecrated in 1258) and Chartres (right) in France (dedicated in 1260) took many years to construct and they still dominate their landscapes. Built to the glory of God, their vertical elements such as spires and high naves were designed to draw the worshiper's eyes to heaven, encourage prayer, and convey a sense of the majesty of God. Their stained glass, sculpture, and paintings were created to teach the stories of the Bible.

the Catholic Church discouraged its translation into vernacular languages. The few vernacular translations that did appear came from groups that were considered heretics or—equally bad in the eyes of the church—reformers. In 1199, Pope Innocent III banned unauthorized versions of the Bible in response to translations used by the French Cathars and the Waldensians.

Although most people could not read the Bible, they learned its stories and teaching through drama, songs, stories, paintings, tapestry, sculpture, stained glass, and more. Pope Gregory the Great, who died in 604, said, "For what Scripture is to those who can read, a picture offers to the illiterate, . . . for in it the ignorant see what should be imitated and those who do not understand writing, read from it."[69] Since books had to be copied by hand, they were incredibly scarce, and even kings and nobles who were able to read had clerks who read to them. So it was not unusual that the common person, who could not read anyway, would learn about the Bible from preacher, priest, and minstrel.

DRAMA - In the early Middle Ages the mass itself was seen as a drama, and on special occasions, such as Palm Sunday, reenactments of Bible stories would fill an entire town. The most famous such drama, although not from the Middle Ages, is an all-day Passion Play. In 1633 the people of Oberammergau, Germany, said that if God spared them from the bubonic plague, they would perform a play every ten years depicting the life and death of Jesus. Very few died, and the citizens kept their word, performing the first play in 1634, and it continues today.

ART - Churches and monasteries were filled with paintings, mosaics, and sculptures depicting biblical characters and stories. Elaborate golden mosaics—enough to cover a football field—fill St. Mark's Basilica in Venice, Italy. Paintings of the stories from the Pentateuch dominate Saint-Savin Abbey church in

France: creation, Adam and Eve, the Tower of Babel, and the stories of Noah, Abraham, Joseph, and Moses.

POETRY - Most medieval poetry retold or expounded on biblical stories and themes. The greatest is Dante's *Divine Comedy*. Written in the fourteenth century in Italian, it tells of Dante's journey through hell, purgatory, and paradise. Although entirely fiction, Dante's *Inferno* has probably done as much to form people's view of hell as has the Bible itself.

ARCHITECTURE - The most obvious evidence of the wealth of the church and local civic pride was the magnificent cathedrals built in the Middle Ages: Chartres and Notre Dame in France, for instance, Aachen and Cologne in Germany, St. Peter's and St. Mark's in Italy, Toledo and Seville in Spain, and Salisbury, Lincoln, and Westminster cathedrals in England. Through sculpture, painting, stained glass, and the architecture itself, cathedrals were designed to point the worshiper to God and the Bible. These buildings were huge and cost an immense amount of time and money. Cathedrals were built for the glory of God, but pride and envy were undoubtedly motivating factors as well. The sale of indulgences to help finance the construction of St. Peter's in Rome led to Martin Luther's ninety-five theses, which led to the Protestant Reformation.

Churches and cathedrals were usually dedicated to a saint and, if possible, contained a relic related to the saint because the presence of relics would attract pilgrims—and donations. There was a hierarchy of saints: Mary, queen of heaven, was at the top; the apostles next; followed by local saints. The obvious problem was that it was far easier to acquire a relic of a local saint—perhaps even the remains of an entire body—than a relic of a more universal saint.[70] The demand for relics was high and "a fantastic assortment of bones, stray bits of timber thought to be fragments of the True Cross, and the like, were reverently preserved."[71] "When . . . relics were stolen, invented, altered, or multiplied, pious devotion and criminal fraud—and every shade of the spectrum between—were inextricably mingled."[72]

THE MIDDLE AGES WAS ALSO WHEN MAGNIFICENT illuminated Bibles, some of the world's greatest artistic masterpieces, were created. These Bibles contained illustrations, decorative initials, and designs frequently using gold or silver painted on parchment or vellum. Many of the eleventh- and twelfth-century illuminated Bibles were large and bound in several volumes. The biggest, *Codex Gigas*, also called the Devil's Bible, is three feet tall, 20" wide, weighs nearly 165 pounds, and used vellum from 160 animals. In the thirteenth century smaller Bibles were made that were much more portable—about the same size as Bibles today.

ALTHOUGH MOST PEOPLE COULD NOT READ THE BIBLE, they learned its stories . . . through drama, songs, stories, paintings, tapestry, sculpture, stained glass, and more.

Thousands of illuminated Bibles still exist, many with fascinating stories of their creation and history. When the prohibition against using "graven images" was lifted in Constantinople in 843, art flourished, including some wonderful illuminated manuscripts. Two of the most outstanding examples are the Joshua Roll,[73] a masterpiece containing the book of Joshua in a scroll instead of a codex, and the Paris

70 According to tradition, the gospel writer Mark founded the church in Alexandria, Egypt. In AD 68 he was tied to horses and dragged through the streets until dead. He was buried in the church, but in 828 two merchants from Venice, Italy, took the body to Venice, although Mark's head remained in Alexandria and once a year was brought out to celebrate the founding of the church there. For more than 1,100 years the headless body was the most honored relic in Venice's magnificent St. Mark's Basilica until June, 1968, when Pope Paul VI returned the body to Alexandria where it and the head could be reunited.

71 Brooke and Brooke, *Popular Religion in the Middle Ages*, 14.

72 Ibid., 17.

73 The Joshua Roll is in the Vatican Library.

74 The Paris Psalter is in the Bibliotèque Nationale de France.

75 The Crusader's Bible is in the Pierpont Morgan Library in New York.

76 De Hamel, *The Book: A History of The Bible*, 151.

77 Codex Aureus (St. Emmeram) is in the Bavarian State Library in Munich, Germany.

78 De Hamel, *The Book: A History of The Bible*, 80.

79 The Winchester Bible is in the Winchester Cathedral in England.

Throughout history artists have depicted biblical characters dressed as contemporaries of the artist. Some of the most interesting examples are the pictures in the Crusader's Bible, made in the thirteenth century. This picture of Saul and his men slaying Nahash and the Ammonites (see 1 Samuel 11:11.) pictures them with medieval armor, weapons, and battle formations. Particularly interesting is the soldier hanging from the catapult in the left margin and the soldier with a recurve bow in a castle tower at the top. The Crusader's Bible is in the Pierpont Morgan Library in New York.

Psalter,[74] which contains fourteen full-page miniatures and was taken to Paris in the sixteenth century.

THE CRUSADER'S BIBLE,[75] painted between 1244 and 1254 in Paris as a picture Bible for King Louis IX of France, tells the Old Testament story from the creation of the world to King David. Originally it had no words—only two to four pictures per page. Explanations were added by various owners in Latin, Persian (in 1604 the pope gave the book to Shah Abbas of Persia), and Hebrew. "It is one of the most beautiful and elegant Gothic manuscripts in existence."[76]

CODEX AUREUS (ST. EMMERAM) was commissioned in 870 by Charles the Bald, grandson of Charlemagne and himself emperor. It contains the text of the four gospels, and the book's lavish opulence seems designed to show the wealth and power of Charles. The cover contains a relief in gold of Christ surrounded by gold, jewels, and pearls. One of the book's seven full-page pictures is of Charles himself; another is the twenty-four elders from Revelation 4—along with Charles—in adoration of the Lamb of God.[77]

THE WINCHESTER BIBLE, one of the greatest works of art ever produced in England,[78] is a large Bible originally bound in two volumes. The text was probably written by a single scribe, but the illustrations, which are still unfinished, were created by a series of artists over several decades. Particularly fascinating are the initial letters. One "P," for instance, contains the prophet Elijah being taken up into heaven and includes chariots of fire pulled by horses.[79]

TWO OF THE MOST SPECTACULAR ILLUMINATED gospels were both created in the British Isles: the Lindisfarne Gospels in northern England and the Book of Kells, Ireland's finest national treasure, was begun in Scotland and completed in Ireland.

Christianity came to Britain when the Romans extended their empire to the British Isles in the first century. The Vikings then invaded Britain and drove Christianity to the western and northern areas—Ireland and Scotland—until Saint Augustine (a different Saint Augustine from the Bishop of Hippo who wrote his *Confessions*) arrived from Rome in 597 to convert the "Angles into angels." Christianity has a history in Britain that goes back nearly two thousand years.

Remarkably well preserved, the Lindisfarne Gospels is the work of Eadfrith, Bishop of Lindisfarne in the eighth century. About two hundred years later, Aldred, self-described as an unworthy and most miserable priest, inserted in red ink between the lines of Latin an Old English translation of the gospels, which is the earliest known English translation of any portion of the Bible.

Viking raids, which began in 793, eventually forced the monks to abandon their island of Lindisfarne in 875. They took with them the body of Saint Cuthbert and, presumably, the Lindisfarne Gospels. According to legend, the dead Saint Cuthbert revealed that he wanted his body to rest in Durham, where the beautiful Romanesque Durham Cathedral was later built to house his shrine. In the sixteenth century, the book was seized by commissioners of King Henry VIII and taken to the Tower of London. The Lindisfarne Gospels later became part of the Cotton Library and is currently in the British Library.

Each of the gospels has a portrait of the writer, followed by a "carpet page," so-called because an intricate pattern covers the entire page. It is an astonishingly beautiful work of art, using forty-two different colors and shades,[80] and is important because it helped build a growing sense of English national identity.

The Book of Kells also contains the four gospels in Latin. It was created about AD 800, probably begun by monks in a monastery founded by Saint Columba on the island of Iona off the western coast of Scotland. Viking raids caused the monks to flee for Ireland's Abbey at Kells. The book was completed there, stolen for two months in 1006 when it lost some pages and its cover, and in 1661 was presented to the Library of Trinity College, Dublin, where it is still on display.

The hand lettering in the Book of Kells is of finest quality, and the illumination is spectacular. Although it does not use gold or silver, the artists "made extravagant use of lapis lazuli, a semi-precious stone from Afghanistan and considered to be as priceless as gold."[81] In the twelfth century Gerald of Wales described what was probably the Book of Kells: "For almost every page there are different designs, distinguished by varied colors. . . . Fine craftsmanship is all about you, but you might not notice it. Look more keenly at it and you will penetrate to the very shrine of art. You will make out intricacies, so delicate and so subtle, so full of knots and links, with colors so fresh and vivid, that you might say that all this were the work of an angel, and not of a man."[82]

The decorations are extremely complex and so intricate that they can be seen best only with a magnifying glass, which was not available when the book was created. The opening few words of each gospel are so lavish and elaborate that the text itself is almost illegible. In contrast to the East, aesthetics were generally given priority over utility in the West.

With the Bible at the center of medieval thought and culture, it should be no surprise that the artistic spirit of the Middle Ages focused on the Bible and its stories. Like the majestic cathedrals, illuminated Bibles were created for the glory of God, and both the cathedrals and illuminated Bibles are a testimony to the importance people placed on their worship and honor of God.

80 Ingo F. Walther and Norbert Wolf, *Masterpieces of Illumination: The World's Most Beautiful Illuminated Manuscripts 400-1600*, (Koln: Taschen, 2005), 70.
81 Ibid., 80.
82 http://en.wikipedia.org/wiki/Book_of_Kells, (accessed August 27, 2009).
83 B. F. Westcott, *A General View of the History of the English Bible*, rev. William Aldis Wright, (London: Macmillan, 1905), 12.

BY THE FOURTEENTH AND FIFTEENTH CENTURIES, the leadership of the church had become divided and contentious, abuses of indulgences grew, the Black Plague wiped out one-third of Europe's population, and individual nations began to establish their national identities, thereby reducing the political importance of the church and the pope. The Renaissance was born in northern Italy, with Michelangelo, da Vinci, and a host of other creative geniuses. It was a period of pestilence, famine, and war, and "widespread disorganization of society."[83]

The influence of the Roman Church had become as much political as spiritual. The Crusades solidified the pope's political authority, even over kings. The resulting power and prosperity of the papacy brought corruption and encouraged efforts by the pope to control and suppress his opponents, who could be threatened with excommunication and even death. In response to the church's prosperity, groups of friars were formed who owned nothing and lived by the generosity of others. Most notable were the Franciscans and Dominicans.

Into this world was born John Wycliffe in the 1320s in northern England. He studied mathematics, natural science, and theology at Oxford University. An excellent student and speaker, he became a teacher, then a preacher, and finally became involved in politics as both a patriot and a reformer.

The more Wycliffe thought about how the church was corrupted by power and prosperity, the more he wanted to cause change, and so he began writing tracts and books. The church, he said, should be poor like the church of the first century instead of rich as the result of commissions, extractions, the abuse of indulgences, and squandering of donations by unfit priests.

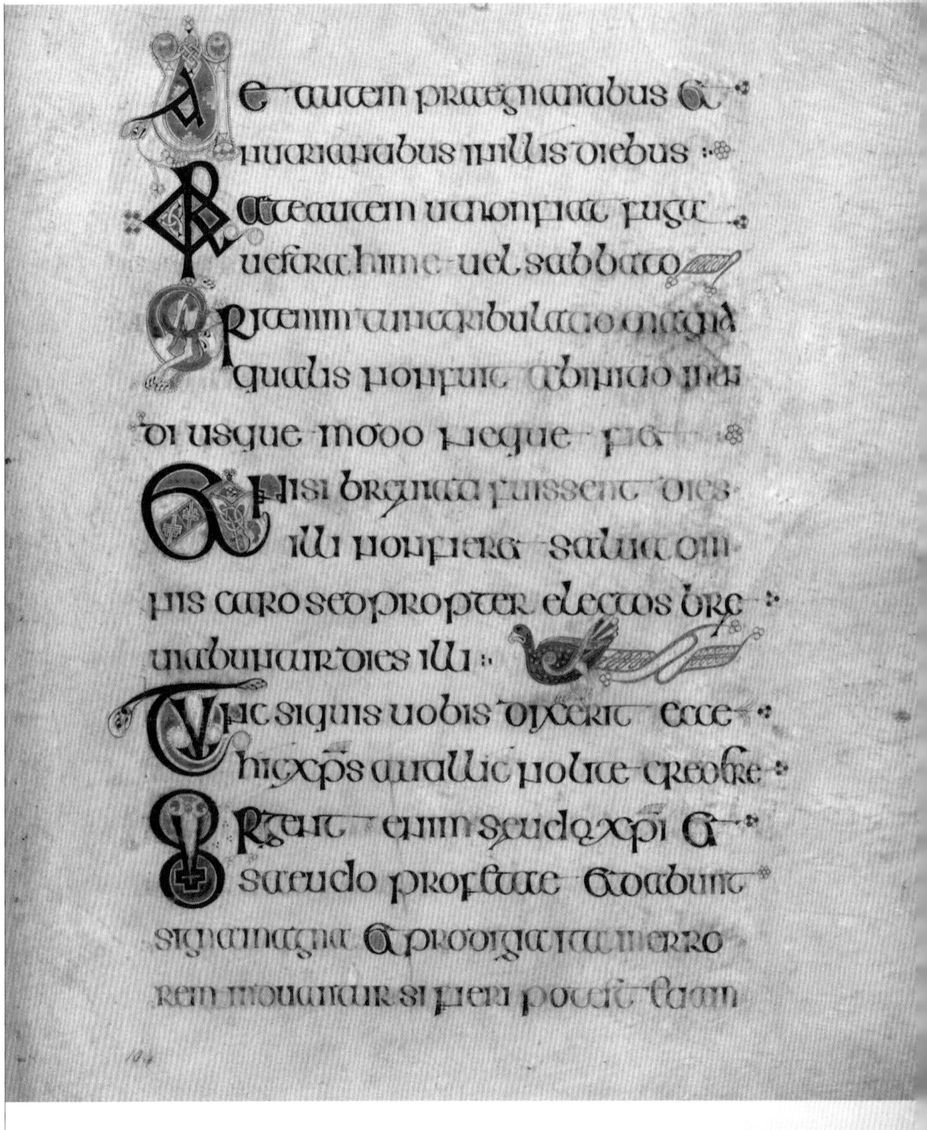

Although the Book of Kells is one of the most beautiful medieval works of art, it is foremost a portion of the New Testament and the art exists to decorate the gospels. This page contains Matthew 24:19-24. Each sentence, (they correspond with our verses) starts with an elaborate letter or two. In Latin, the first word in verse 19 is "vae." The "v" and "a" are combined before the "e". Verse 20 begins with "orate," verse 21 with "erit," verse 22 with "et nisi," verse 23 with "tunc," and verse 24 with "sugent." It is interesting to examine the ways the initial letters are drawn. The Book of Kells is in Trinity College Library, Dublin.

Not surprisingly, Wycliffe's teachings were vigorously opposed by the church. The more the church protested his teachings, the more adamant Wycliffe became that the property of the church should be put in the hands of the people and the church reformed. He said the only authority is Scripture, a statement that later became a core principle of the Reformation, causing Wycliffe to be called "The Morning Star of the Reformation."

Wycliffe sent out itinerant preachers called Lollards, who went two by two, barefoot, wearing long dark red robes, and preaching the gospel, the importance of piety, and the teachings of Wycliffe. The church declared Lollards to be heretics. Some were burned alive for their beliefs and the political implications of their teachings.

With Wycliffe and the Lollards advocating the authority of Scripture, he naturally wanted to see the entire Bible translated into English. Also, because the Bible was already available to nobility in French, the honor of England demanded an English translation. One hundred fifty years later, the English Bible "would be seen as a symbol of national pride and international status."[84] The translation of the Bible into English made sense both spiritually and politically.

Wycliffe completed a translation of the New Testament from Latin, and Nicholas de Hereford, a friend, translated much of the Old Testament, also from Latin, until he was excommunicated and left England. After Wycliffe completed de Hereford's Old Testament translation, the entire Bible was then revised by John Purvey.[85]

Wycliffe continued to write, speak, and preach about the imperfections of the church. "Wycliffe thus threatened to destroy the whole edifice of clerical domination in matters of theology and church life. The translation of the Bible into English would be a social leveler on a hitherto unknown scale."[86] John Wycliffe suffered a stroke and died on December 31, 1384. In 1415 the Council of Constance declared him to be "a stiff-necked heretic" and decreed that his books be burned. Thirteen years later, at the command of Pope Martin V, Wycliffe's bones were dug up, burned, and the ashes thrown into England's River Swift. About 250 copies of Wycliffe's translation survive, most as Purvey's revision.

In 1408 at Canterbury under Archbishop Arundel, it was "decree[d] and ordain[ed] that no man hereafter by his own authority translate any text of the Scripture into English or any other tongue, . . . and that no man read any such book, pamphlet, or treatise now lately composed in the time of John Wycliffe or since . . . upon pain of greater excommunication, until the said translation be approved by the ordinary of the place." Not only was this an effort to maintain the power of the church, but it was also based on the idea that "English was a barbarous language, lacking any real grammatical structure, incapable of expressing the deep and nuanced truths of the Bible."[87]

Archbishop Arundel might have thought he won the battle, but Wycliffe won the war. The world was ready for a change. There was a hunger for access to the Bible just as there was a hunger for political and ecclesiastical freedom. "The Morning Star of the Reformation" opened the Bible so that English-speaking people could read that salvation comes by faith. But it was left to Martin Luther and others one hundred fifty years later to bring reformation to the hearts and minds of many throughout Europe.

84 Alister E. McGrath, *In the Beginning: The Story of the King James Bible and How it Changed a Nation, a Language, and a Culture*, (New York: Doubleday, 2001), 36.

85 In the introduction to his revision of the Wycliffe Bible, John Purvey said the translator of Scripture "hath need to live a clean life and be full devout in prayers, and have not his wit occupied about worldly things, that the Holy Spirit . . . dress him for his works and suffer him not to err."

86 McGrath, *In the Beginning*, 19.

87 Ibid., 33.

THE OLDEST BIBLE WITH VOWELS

The twenty-two letters of the Hebrew alphabet are all consonants. Reading a text without vowels is not that hard to do, and even modern Hebrew is written without vowels. For instance, "Th lttl chld s cryng n th bdrm" is easy to read. Moreover, in Old Testament times a scribe could repeat an entire book accurately from memory.

After the Jews returned from captivity, they were less familiar with Hebrew, which is why the Old Testament was translated into Greek and Aramaic. In AD 70 the Romans destroyed Jerusalem, and in 135 they quashed another Jewish revolt and forced many to leave their land or sold them as slaves. Many Jews no longer spoke Hebrew and had difficulty reading Scripture.

The Masoretes (from a Hebrew word meaning "tradition") were scholars and scribes who guarded and preserved the Hebrew text of the Bible. The Jews living outside Palestine read the Greek Septuagint or the Aramaic targums, but there were "substantial differences"[88] among them, and so the Masoretes reviewed the variant readings and made determinations of what every word and every letter in the Bible should be.

In about AD 500, Jewish scribes in Babylon developed a system of adding vowels to Hebrew, and later Masoretes improved the system of what is called vowel points. For instance one dot under a letter is an "i"; two dots under a letter is a short "e", a short line under a letter is a short "a." We know the Masoretic Text accurately represents the Old Testament from at least 100 BC because of comparisons with the Dead Sea Scrolls.

Between the eighth and tenth centuries Tiberias, a town on the shore of the Sea of Galillee, became the center of a community of masoretic scholars, including the ben Asher family. In about 930 Aaron ben Asher took a complete manuscript of the Old Testament, proofread it, and added vowel points and masoretic commentary. Until the discovery of the Dead Sea Scrolls, Aaron ben Asher's manuscript, the Aleppo Codex, was the earliest complete Hebrew manuscript of the Old Testament in existence. For more than one thousand years, it was carefully preserved in Tiberias, Jerusalem, Egypt, and finally in Aleppo in Syria.

Riots broke out in Syria in 1947 when the United Nations established the State of Israel and the codex disappeared. Someone kept it in a secret hiding place, but even so, about one-fourth of it was destroyed or lost. In 1958 what remained of the Aleppo Codex was smuggled out of Syria and is now preserved in The Shrine of the Book in Jerusalem.

Efforts to discover the missing parts of the codex have not been successful, with the exception of a full page from 2 Chronicles and a fragment of a page from Exodus. Both were discovered in Brooklyn, New York, owned by people who had previously lived in Aleppo.

(Above) The top part of the page in the Aleppo Codex containing Psalm 119:122 to 119:170. Each eight lines (our verses) from Psalm 119 starts with the same letter in the Hebrew alphabet. Each of the seven lines at the top right (the beginning of the page) starts at the right with the Hebrew ayin (ע); the next eight lines below it start with pe (פ); this is followed by the first of eight lines beginning with tsadhe (צ); qoph (ק) at the top of the left column is next; followed by resh (ר); and then the first of eight lines that begin with shin (ש).

88 William White Jr., "Introduction," in *Nelson's Expository Dictionary of the Old Testament*, (Nashville: Thomas Nelson Publishers, 1980), xi.

6

THE REMARKABLE CENTURY FROM GUTENBERG TO LUTHER

BETWEEN 1450 AND 1550 THE WORLD CHANGED.

The invention of printing cut the cost of information to a fraction of what it had been when books were written by hand. Literacy exploded. And because books were printed in everyday languages people spoke—not just in Latin—learning and education became widespread, which made the Scientific Revolution possible. Languages became more uniform, leading to easier communication. Easier communication helped trade, which then grew in importance.

The medieval feudal system had concentrated power and wealth in a small number of families, but the increasing role of merchants, entrepreneurs, and traders led to a growing middle class. Individual countries in Europe developed a stronger sense of nationalism. They also took steps to make sure money stayed in the country rather than go to the pope, whether by taxes or indulgences.[89] Kings realized they no longer had to be subservient to the pope. (In England the process was helped along by Henry VIII's libido, ego, and desire for a male heir.) The Vatican's political, economic, ecclesiastical, and intellectual domination of Europe was ending. Also during this 100-year period Christopher Columbus discovered the New World, Ferdinand Magellan sailed around the world, and Copernicus said that the sun, not the earth, is the center of the universe.

At the center of this change in literacy, in education, in politics, and in economics was the Bible. During these one hundred years there were four significant developments in the story of the Bible:

[89] Luther wrote, "Some have estimated that every year more than 300,000 gulden find their way from Germany to Italy. . . . How comes it that we Germans must put up with such robbery and such extortion of our property at the hands of the pope?" (Will Durant [*The Reformation*, vol. 6 in *The Story of Civilization*], 353).

Before Gutenberg, each book had to be painstakingly copied by hand. After Gutenberg determined a metal alloy for type, developed an oil-based ink, and adapted a wine or olive press to printing, thousands of books could be printed at a time. Before Gutenberg, culture and knowledge were reserved for the educated and wealthy; after Gutenberg, books were available to anyone who could read. This twentieth-century illustration shows Gutenberg examining a newly printed page in his Mainz print shop.

- The invention of printing made the Bible more widely available.
- Widespread translation into spoken languages made the Bible more easily read and understood.
- Interest in translating the Bible from Greek and Hebrew made the translated Bibles more accurate and authoritative.
- The Reformation declared the Bible to be supreme authority, not the pope and the church.

The two key people in this seismic change in the world were both Germans: Johannes Gutenberg and Martin Luther.

WE KNOW LITTLE ABOUT THE PERSONAL LIFE OF Johannes Gutenberg, whom *Time* magazine chose in 1999 as "the Man of the Millennium." Gutenberg was born as Johann Gensfleisch (John Gooseflesh) of a well-to-do family near Mainz, Germany, and became a goldsmith or gem cutter in Strasbourg, where he also became involved in printing. Printing presses at the time used individually carved wooden blocks to transfer ink to paper. This was useful for printing handbills, playing cards, and pictures of saints, but not practical for books.

In 1448 Gutenberg returned to Mainz, set up a print shop, and helped fill a huge market for printed certificates of indulgences, acknowledgments of a gift to the church in exchange for forgiveness of the punishment of sins. He also developed a process for printing books using movable type. He chose a metal alloy for the type that would melt at a relatively low temperature but would withstand the pressure of the printing press. He developed an oil-based ink that would transfer best to paper. Gutenberg's inventions seem obvious today, but at the time they were revolutionary. For each page of a book, a typesetter would select the letters and arrange them in a frame, which was then locked in the bed of a press that had been adapted from a wine or olive press.

Vniuersis ... Paulinus ...

Forma plenissime absolutionis et remissionis in vita

Misereatur tui ...

Forma plenarie remissionis in mortis articulo

Misereatur tui ...

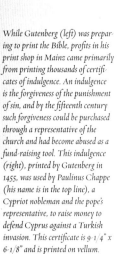

While Gutenberg (left) was preparing to print the Bible, profits in his print shop in Mainz came primarily from printing thousands of certificates of indulgence. An indulgence is the forgiveness of the punishment of sin, and by the fifteenth century such forgiveness could be purchased through a representative of the church and had become abused as a fund-raising tool. This indulgence (right), printed by Gutenberg in 1455, was used by Paulinus Chappe (his name is in the top line), a Cypriot nobleman and the pope's representative, to raise money to defend Cyprus against a Turkish invasion. This certificate is 9-1/4" x 6-1/8" and is printed on vellum.

The type was inked with horsehair-stuffed balls, and a sheet of paper was moistened, placed on the inked type, and pressed down.

Before Gutenberg, each book had to be painstakingly hand copied; after Gutenberg, a book could be printed thousands of times. It was said of another printer, "He prints as much in a day as was formerly written in a year."[90] Before Gutenberg, culture and knowledge were reserved for the educated and wealthy; after Gutenberg, it was made available to anyone who could read. Before Gutenberg, libraries were small—the Cambridge University Library had only 122 volumes in 1424, for instance; after Gutenberg, literacy became widespread.

Gutenberg's masterpiece was a Bible, and his goal was to reproduce the look of a handwritten manuscript by the printing press. It was a huge financial investment. It is estimated that he would have had to create 100,000 individual pieces of type,[91] and what he made were beautiful replicas of the calligrapher's skill. He would also have had to buy paper and vellum. (Each Bible printed on vellum required the skins of more than 160 animals.) In 1450 he borrowed 800 guilders from Johann Faust, a rich goldsmith. In 1454 and again in 1455, he or an associate displayed copies of printed pages of a Bible at gatherings in Frankfurt so that he could sell the Bibles before they were printed. Sales were strong enough so that the initial printing of about 130 copies was increased to about 180. The publication of those 180 Bibles changed the world!

"It is often assumed that [Gutenberg] invented printing and then looked about for a major text to publish . . . and that he opted for the Bible. It could as well be the other way round," speculates Christopher de Hamel. "Perhaps he perceived a market for Bibles and pondered how to supply them in large numbers."[92]

Gutenberg's Bible was in Latin, about 11-1/2" x 16", in two volumes totaling 1,282 pages. It was printed in two columns of forty-two lines each in black (a few copies have some headings in red) with space left for colored additions. Each Bible is different

90 David Wright, "The Reformation to 1700," in *The Oxford Illustrated History of the Bible*, ed. John Rogerson, (Oxford: Oxford University Press, 2001), 193.

91 C. Singer, E. Holmyard, A. Hall, and T. Williams, *A History of Technology*, vol. 3, (Oxford: Oxford University Press, 1958).

92 De Hamel, *The Book: The History of The Bible*, 194.

93 Harry Thomas Frank, Charles William Swain, and Courtlandt Canby, *The Bible through the Ages* (Cleveland: World Publishing, 1967), 59, quoted in Donald L. Brake, *A Visual History of the English Bible* (Grand Rapids: Baker Books, 2008), 79.

94 Durant, *The Reformation*, 159.

95 Jean Mary Stone, *Reformation and Renaissance (circa 1377-1610)* (London: Duckworth, 1904), 453-456.

96 Durant, *The Reformation*, 160.

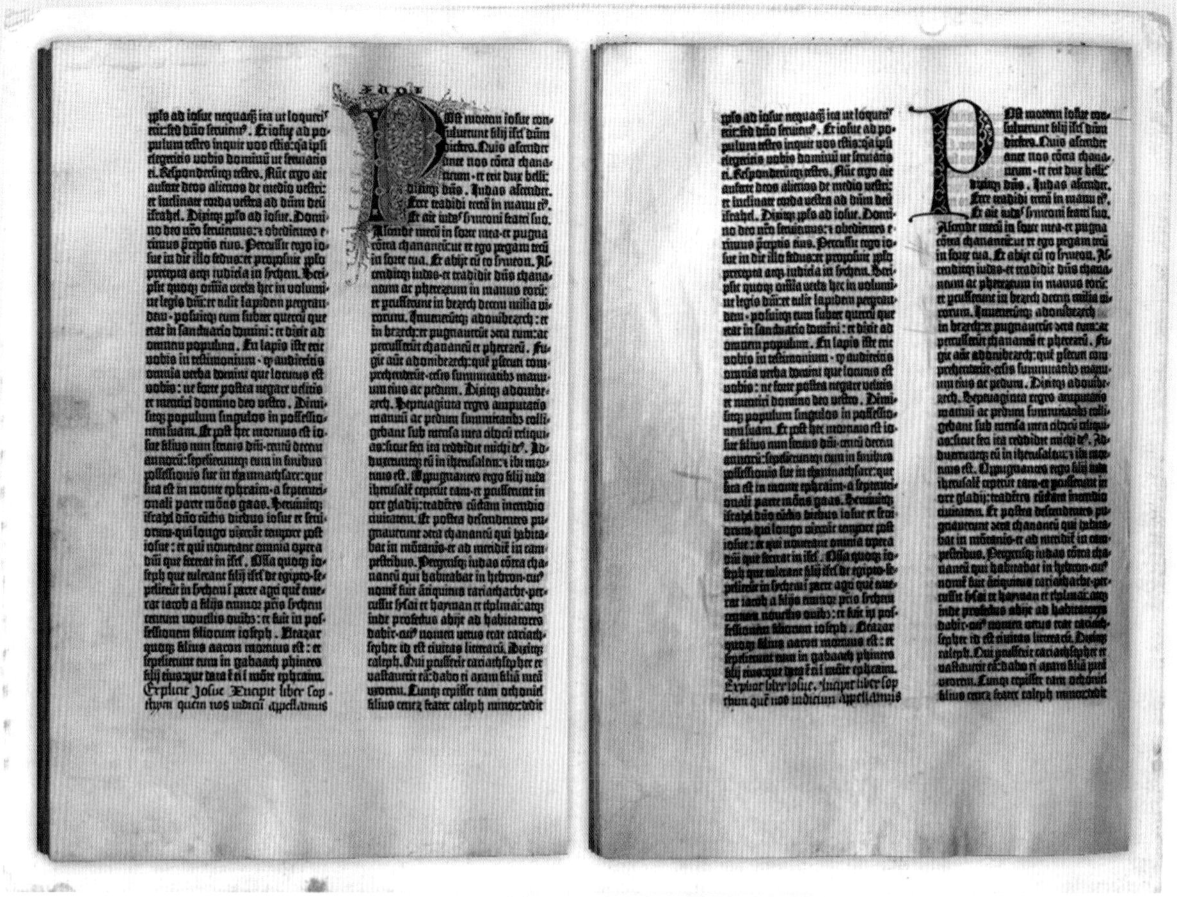

Because Gutenberg's goal was to reproduce the look of a medieval manuscript, he printed the Bible in black ink with space for colored additions. Each Bible is different; the amount of decoration in a Bible depended on how much the owner wanted to spend. Compare the removable document page with the same page from two Gutenberg Bibles at the British Library. The page on the left is from a copy printed on paper, known as the King's copy; the page on the right is from a copy printed on vellum, known as Grenville's copy. The last two lines in the left column and the initial "P" in the right column are different in all three Bibles. Those parts were made by hand. The rest of the type, however, is identical.

because the decoration of each was individually hand colored. Forty-eight copies still exist, and they are the world's most valuable printed books.

Gutenberg's invention did not bring him financial success. In fact, he was unable to repay Faust, who took over the print shop, the presses, and the type.

The making of books with movable type spread rapidly. By 1500 presses had been set up in Rome, Paris, Venice, Constantinople, Holland, Switzerland, Hungary, Spain, England, Denmark, and Sweden, and an estimated thirty-thousand titles had been published, more copies of books in fifty years than had been produced in all of prior human history.[93] "A passion for books became one of the effervescent ingredients of the Reformation age," says Will Durant, and he quotes a letter from a scholar in Basel, Germany, to a friend: "A whole wagon load of classics . . . has arrived from Venice. Do you want any? . . . .No sooner is such a freight landed than thirty buyers rise up for each volume, merely asking the price, and tearing one another's eyes out to get hold of them."[94]

The printing press encouraged the distribution of the Bible in vernacular languages. The first complete Old Testament in Hebrew was printed in Soncino, Italy, in 1488. In 1877 the British Museum had an exhibit of Bibles and testaments in Latin, German, Italian, French, Dutch, Hebrew, and Bohemian—all printed before 1500.[95] Medieval Bibles were expensive, scarce, and in a language only the educated understood. By 1500 Bibles were available to thousands who could not have read them before Gutenberg. "Printing," says Will Durant, "paved the way for the Enlightenment, for the American and French revolutions, for democracy."[96]

Born in 1483, Martin Luther never knew a time when there were no printed books. He graduated from the University of Erfurt, and when he was nearly struck by a lightening bolt, he became an Augustinian

Martin Luther, German priest, professor of theology, translator, and father of the Reformation. His teachings replaced the authority of the church with the authority of the Bible; his translation gave Germans the means to read the Bible for themselves.

monk. His awareness of his own sinfulness led him to long hours of prayer and fasting.

The Roman Church taught that to absolve one's sins, that person's faith had to be demonstrated by good works—such as giving money to the church. This teaching became corrupted into the sale of indulgences both for one's own sins as well as for the sins of others. "As soon as the money in the coffer rings, the soul from purgatory's fire springs," it was said. When Pope Leo X raised money for the completion of St. Peter's basilica in Rome through the sale of indulgences, Luther raised ninety-five questions about the practice, which he put on the church door in Wittenberg, Germany, on October 31, 1517. One of those questions was, "Why does not the pope, whose wealth is today greater than the riches of the richest, build just this one church of St. Peter with his own money, rather than with the money of poor believers?"

The church was slow to respond to Luther's questions, and the division between the church and Luther widened with a little name-calling on both sides. The pope described Luther as "a drunken German" who "when sober will change his mind," and Luther said the pope was "the real Anti-Christ of whom all Scripture speaks." Luther wanted to stay in the church and reform it, but he was excommunicated in 1521.

The differences between the church and the reformers—Luther, John Calvin, Ulrich Zwingli, and others—grew beyond just the abuse of indulgences and are summarized in the "Five Solas" of the Reformation: Sola Fide ("by faith alone," meaning salvation comes by faith, not by good works such as buying indulgences); Sola Scriptura ("by Scripture alone," meaning that Scripture, not the church or pope, is the ultimate authority and that it can be read by all); Sola Gratia ("by Grace alone," meaning salvation comes by God's grace or unmerited favor); Solus Christus ("by Christ alone," meaning that Christ is the only mediator between God and man); and Soli Deo Gloria ("Glory to God alone," meaning that glory is due only to God, not to popes or saints). These statements were not just theological distinctives, but a vigorous challenge to the political and ecclesiastical power of the papacy.

After hearing about his excommunication, some of Luther's followers kidnapped him and took him for his own safety to Wartburg Castle near Eisenach, Germany. While there he began translating the New Testament into German from Erasmus's Greek text and the Old Testament from a 1494 copy of the Hebrew Old Testament printed in Soncino.

97 Wright, "The Reformation to 1700," 201.
98 McGrath, *In the Beginning*, 53.
99 De Hamel, *The Book: The History of The Bible*, 218.

The New Testament was published in 1522 and the complete Bible in 1534 with 184 woodcuts. German translations had been made before, but Luther's was readable and contemporary and helped standardize a language that was fragmented by many dialects. "I endeavored to make Moses so German," said Luther, "that no one would suspect he was a Jew."[97] His translation is the finest work in the German language, according to Friedrich Nietzche. Like the King James Version, Luther's Bible is a literary classic that helped to define the language—and, like the King James Version, it is still in use today.

The pope banned Luther's writings, but with little effect. Within fifty years one printer in Wittenburg was said to have printed almost one hundred thousand copies of Luther's translation of the Bible. Letting people read the Bible for themselves was as much about politics and power as about personal spirituality, explains Alister McGrath: "Pressure for the Bible to be placed in the hands of the ordinary person was an implicit demand for the emancipation of the laity from clerical domination."[98] In addition to the Bible, more than 3,700 editions of Luther's books and pamphlets were published in his lifetime.

BETWEEN 1450 AND 1550 THE WORLD CHANGED. . . . The two key people . . . were both Germans: Johannes Gutenberg and Martin Luther.

Four years after posting his ninety-five theses, Luther was summoned to an assembly at the German town of Worms to renounce his writings. "Unless I am convinced by the testimonies of the Holy Scriptures or evident reason," he said, "here I stand; I can do no other. God help me." After he left the meeting, Emperor Charles V issued the Edict of Worms, which said, "We want [Luther] to be apprehended and punished as a notorious heretic, as he deserves."

Luther's translation of the Bible inspired others. Translations were soon made into French, Dutch, Italian, Spanish, Portuguese, Danish, Norwegian, Swedish, Icelandic, Hungarian, Bohemian, Polish, Russian, and modern Greek. Sometimes two translations were made: a Catholic-approved translation made from Latin and a Protestant translation made from Greek and Hebrew. Various translations also reflected the beliefs of the translators. In Matthew 3:2, for instance, John the Baptist said (according to the NKJV), "Repent, for the kingdom of heaven is at hand!" Catholic translators tended to render John's first word as "Do penance," a physical activity required by the church. Protestant translators tended to render the word as "Be penitent," a spiritual turning to God.

"As the battle lines between the Protestants and Catholics became more inflexible, the Catholic camp was reluctantly forced backwards into defending the authenticity of the Vulgate, . . . a position [that] was indefensible."[99] Protestants made the most out

After his refusal to recant at the Diet of Worms, Luther was seized by Prince Frederick of Saxony and, for his own safety, was hidden in Wartburg, a castle overlooking Eisenach. He stayed there from May 1521 until March 1522, when he returned to Wittenberg to help calm disturbances in the town. While at Wartburg Luther completed his translation of the New Testament into German in this room.

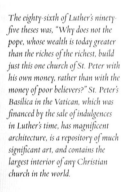

The eighty-sixth of Luther's ninety-five theses was, "Why does not the pope, whose wealth is today greater than the riches of the richest, build just this one church of St. Peter with his own money, rather than with the money of poor believers?" St. Peter's Basilica in the Vatican, which was financed by the sale of indulgences in Luther's time, has magnificent architecture, is a repository of much significant art, and contains the largest interior of any Christian church in the world.

of the fact that their translations were from Greek and Hebrew and therefore closer to the original than translations made from the Vulgate. Although common people did not speak Latin, use of the language was not isolated to the church. Latin was also the universal language of higher learning. Teaching at Oxford and Cambridge was done in Latin, for instance, and the area around the University of Paris became known as the Latin Quarter because that was the language spoken there.

Because people could now read the Bible for themselves, the Roman Church's position that it alone could interpret Scripture was weakened. A disagreement between Luther and Zwingli over what Christ meant when He referred to the bread in the Last Supper as "my body" gave ammunition for the argument that the church should be the final interpreter of Scripture. Left to the judgement of individuals, the Bible could be subjected to a thousand viewpoints and Christianity divided into a thousand sects.[100]

In response to the Reformation, the pope called the Council of Trent, which met three times between 1545 and 1563. "Its main object," according to *The Catholic Encyclopedia*, "was the definitive determination of the doctrines of the Church in answer to the heresies of the Protestants."[101] Among other things, the Council confirmed that the church alone had the right to interpret the Bible, that the Latin Vulgate was the definitive translation of the Bible, that the Apocrypha was part of the Old Testament, and that Erasmus (see sidebar on pages 66-67) was an impious heretic and his works were banned.

A new scholarly edition of the Latin Vulgate was commissioned by Pope Sixtus V, but criticisms led to its replacement by a revision in 1592 called the

100 Durant, *The Reformation*, page 936.
101 http://www.newadvent.org/cathen/15030c.htm (accessed August 27, 2009).
102 Wright, "The Reformation to 1700," 215.

"Clementine" edition, which was used for more than three hundred years.

It's interesting how many Bible translations made in the sixteenth and early seventeenth centuries are still in use today: Luther's German Bible (1522/1534), the King James Version English Bible (1611), the Douay-Rheims English Bible (1582/1609-10), Clemintine's Latin Bible (1592), the Reina-Valera Spanish Bible (1569), and Giovanni Diodati's Italian Bible (1603).

BEFORE 1450 THE DOMINANT WORLDVIEW IN THE West was that of the medieval Roman Church, which sought for itself ecclesiastical, political, economic, and intellectual authority. After 1550 there were three competing worldviews. The world had changed.

The Catholic position gave authority to Scripture, but gave equal authority and the responsibility of interpreting Scripture to the church. In effect the church was the ultimate authority.

The Protestant position ascribed authority to Scripture alone. Political authority rested with civil leaders, whether kings or democratically elected rulers; economic authority rested with individuals, a belief that fostered the development of capitalism; and intellectual authority rested with a pious freedom of discovery.

A third position—that of the humanists—had begun to develop in the Italian Renaissance in the fifteenth and sixteenth centuries and emerged full blown in the Enlightenment in the 1700s. Ultimate authority was neither the Bible nor the church, but reason, science, and philosophy. Knowledge was seen as power.

In response to the Reformation, the pope called the Council of Trent, which confirmed that the church alone had the right to interpret the Bible, that the Latin Vulgate was the definitive translation of the Bible, that the Apocrypha was part of the Old Testament, and that Erasmus was an impious heretic and his works were banned. The picture is the official portrait of the 25th session of the Council, December, 1563.

The story of such change is told through the lives of those who caused it, and at the center was the Bible. A plaque in St. Peter's Cathedral in Geneva describes the reformer John Calvin simply as a "Servant of the Word of God." Luther said, "All I have done is to put forth, preach and write the Word of God, and apart from this I have done nothing. While I have been sleeping, or drinking Wittenberg beer . . . it is the Word that has done great things . . . I have done nothing; the Word has done and achieved everything."[102]

THE GREEK NEW TESTAMENT AND TEXTUAL CRITICISM

OR, WHAT ARE THE CRITICAL TEXT AND THE *TEXTUS RECEPTUS* ANYWAY? AND WHO CARES?

Nothing sounds duller than "New Testament textual criticism"—the process of determining the original wording of the Greek New Testament. But in some circles determining which Greek text is closest to the original manuscripts can still arouse as much passion as an Alabama football game.

Imagine that you write a letter to a friend, who then wants to share with others what you have written. Before the days of photocopy machines, your friend would have had to write out copies of your letter. If those who received the copies wanted to share them, they would have to write out copies of the copy. With each copy a spelling or punctuation difference might be introduced or a word or phrase accidentally added or dropped. If someone wanted to find out what you had really said, he would have to look critically at all the copies of your letter he could find.

The task of determining the original text of the gospel of Luke or a letter by Paul is just the same: find all the copies possible and, by using the principles of textual criticism, determine what the original manuscript said.

The text of the Hebrew Old Testament was preserved by the Masoretes—those Jewish scholars who made sure that every word and letter was accurate—and Pope Damasus asked Jerome to create an accurate Latin translation of the Bible because there were so many variations in the Old Latin texts.

These efforts helped preserve the accuracy of the Hebrew Old Testament and the Latin Bible, but there was no similar effort to preserve an accurate Greek text. Early Christians certainly held the writings of the apostles in the highest regard, but slight differences would appear in copies as the years passed. Moreover, for the first 250 years Christian writings were destroyed during various persecutions. In the Middle Ages the Greek text was used primarily by the Eastern church, but "few scholars troubled themselves to question the accuracy of the copies produced." [103]

Of the more than 5,500 manuscripts of the New Testament that exist, more than three hundred are uncials (written in capital letters) from before the ninth century. More than 2,600 are miniscules (written in cursive letters) copied after the ninth century. (The rest are lectionaries, portions arranged for public worship.)

Scholars say these 5,500 New Testament manuscripts can be categorized in several families, each with distinctive readings: (1) About 80 percent come from the Eastern Mediterranean and are called the Byzantine family of texts. They are also called the Syrian text type and—for obvious reasons—the Majority text. (2) Alexandrian manuscripts (also called the Neutral or Egyptian text type) are older and come mainly from Egypt. The fourth-century codices Vaticanus and Sinaiticus are Alexandrian. (3) Another family of manuscripts come from the Western Mediterranean. (4) Caesarean manuscripts are a mixed lot, and some scholars say they are not a real family.

Neil Lightfoot explains that there are more than two hundred thousand differences across the several families of the New Testament manuscripts. "This large number is gained by counting all the variations in all the manuscripts. For example, if one slight variant were to occur in 4,000 different manuscripts, this would amount to 4,000" variations. Lightfoot identifies three kinds of variations: (1) trivial variations of no consequence to the text (the majority of the 200,000); (2) substantial variations of no consequence to the text; (3) substantial variations that have a bearing on the text.[104]

An example of a variation with little consequence is in John 9, where Jesus made a blind man to see and the Jews asked his parents about it. Some manuscripts begin verse 20, "His parents answered them and said." Other manuscripts say, "But his parents answered them and said." Still others say, "His parents answered and said." And still others say, "His parents answered therefore and said." Such variations have almost no impact on the meaning of the verse, but nevertheless they constitute dozens of variations.

Some variations are more significant. For instance Mark 16:9-20 is found in the Byzantine family of manuscripts, but it is not included in either Codex Sinaiticus or Codex Vaticanus, or other very old manuscripts. John 7:53–8:11, the story of the woman caught in adultery, is also found in many more recent manuscripts, but not in Sinaiticus or Vaticanus. Because the King James Version and the New King James Version are translated from the Greek texts that lean heavily on the Byzantine family of manuscripts while most other modern translations such as the New International Version and Revised Standard Version are based on a text that gives more weight to Sinaiticus and Vaticanus, there are variations in these English translations.[105] And these variations lead to passions about the New Testament text.

Interest in determining the accuracy of the Greek text of the New Testament developed about the time of the invention of printing, and there was a race for the publication of the first printed Greek text.

In 1502 Cardinal Francisco Ximenez de Cisneros in Spain, who with his own money founded a university dedicated to the study of Greek, Hebrew, and Latin, brought together a team of scholars who said they used "very ancient and correct" Greek manuscripts to create the Complutensian Polyglot (named after the Roman town of Complutum, the site of Alcala, Spain, where the Bible was printed). The New Testament contained the Vulgate in one column and the Greek text in another; the Old Testament contained the Hebrew text as well as Latin and Greek. The first five books of the Old Testament also contained Aramaic and a second Latin translation. The New Testament was completed in 1514, but its publication was delayed until the pope gave his permission in 1522. It was an excellent piece of scholarship.

When Johannes Froben, a printer in Basel, Switzerland, heard of the Spanish project, he hired Desiderius Erasmus, a Dutch scholar, to create a new edition of the Greek New Testament, and Froben published the first printed Greek New Testament in 1516. Erasmus admitted that the 1516 edition was "rushed into print rather than edited." The manuscripts

103 Frederic Kenyon, *Recent Developments in the Textual Criticism of the Greek Bible*, (Oxford: Oxford University Press, 1933), 2, 3.

104 Lightfoot, *How We Got the Bible*, 95-103.

105 The New International Version, for instance, includes Mark 16:9-20 with the comment, "The two most reliable early manuscripts do not have Mark 16:9-20," and includes John 7:53 – 8:11 with the comment, "The earliest and most reliable manuscripts do not have John 7:53-8:11."

106 Donald Brake, *A Visual History of the English Bible* (Grand Rapids: Baker Books, 2008), 93.

107 In 1519, 1522, 1527, and 1535.

108 This was the same Robert Stephanus who designated the verse divisions in Scripture that are still in use today.

109 Frederic G. Kenyon, *Handbook of the Textual Criticism of the New Testament* (London: Macmillan and Co., 1901), 271.

110 McGrath, *In the Beginning*, 242.

Erasmus, a Dutch scholar, theologian, and humanist, created a Greek text of the New Testament using Byzantine Greek manuscripts. Because of a delay in the publication of the Complutensian Polyglot, his was the first published Greek New Testament. Erasmus published five editions and his Greek text was used as the basis of Luther's and probably Tyndale's New Testaments, and the Geneva and King James Version Bibles.

he consulted were at Basel University and convenient, but not necessarily the most complete. For instance, since the last six verses of Revelation were missing from the Greek manuscripts he consulted, Erasmus translated those six verses from Latin into Greek. Other passages he translated from Latin into Greek do not appear in any Greek manuscripts, but nevertheless show up in some modern translations that are based on Erasmus's Greek text.[106] Over the next twenty years, Erasmus issued four more editions,[107] each correcting misprints and inserting improved readings. Two other sixteenth-century publishers of the Greek text, Robert Stephanus[108] and Theodore Beza, used texts similar to that of Erasmus's fifth edition. These texts were based on the Byzantine family of manuscripts and became known as the "Received Text" (*textus receptus*), which was the Greek text that was used by the King James Version translators.

Not until the nineteenth century did scholars began making judgments on which reading was "best"—which reading the editor thinks is most like the original. In 1831 Karl Lachmann, a German scholar, published the first "critical text" of the New Testament, which accepted some readings and rejected others. Constantine von Tischendorf, who discovered Codex Sinaiticus, did the same a few years later.

The most notable textual critics were Cambridge scholars B. F. Westcott and F. J. A. Hort, who felt that Alexandrian manuscripts from the fourth century, particularly Vaticanus and Sinaiticus, represented the most accurate transmission of the New Testament because, since they were older, they had not yet been subjected to editorial revision by scribes. In 1881 Westcott and Hort published a Greek New Testament based on Alexandrian manuscripts rather than Byzantine manuscripts.

Most scholars today do not adhere as closely to the Alexandrian manuscripts as Westcott and Hort did, but nevertheless believe in the superiority of Vaticanus and Siniaticus and follow an "eclectic" method, by choosing readings (1) that best explain the origin of the different variations, and (2) that the author is most likely to have written. The two most popular editions of the Greek New Testament today—the United Bible Societies edition and the Nestle-Aland Text—are both based on the eclectic method. In 1982 a modern critical edition of the Byzantine family of texts was published by Thomas Nelson Publishers, appropriately called *The Greek New Testament According to the Majority Text*.

But for all the debate on which New Testament text is best, it is good to remember what Frederic Kenyon said in 1901: "The differences between the rival types of text is not one of doctrine. No fundamental point of doctrine rests upon a disputed reading: and the truths of Christianity are as certainly expressed in the text of Westcott and Hort as in that of Stephanus."[109] Alister McGrath made the same point one hundred years later. "We now have access to a much more accurate edition of the text of the [Greek] New Testament than the King James translators knew. It must be made clear immediately that this does not call into question the general reliability of the King James Bible. . . . Not a single teaching of the Christian faith is affected by these variations, nor is any major historical aspect of the gospel narratives or early Christianity affected." [110]

Hæc tibi pentadecas tetragonon respicit illud
Hospitium petri & pauli ter quinqʒ dierum.
Namqʒ instrumētum vetus hebdoas innuit: octo
Lex noua signatur, ter quinqʒ receptat vtrunqʒ.

Vetus testamentū multiplici lingua nūc
primo impressum. Et imprimis
Pentateuchus Hebraico Gre-
co atqʒ Chaldaico idioma-
te. Adiūcta vnicuiqʒ sua
latina interpreta-
tione.

The title page of the Complutensian Polyglot, a masterpiece of scholarship printed between 1514 and 1517 in Spain. The polyglot included the first printed Greek New Testament, but its publication was delayed until the pope gave his approval in 1522.

7

THE BIBLE IN ENGLISH

JOHN COCHLAEUS, AN ENERGETIC ANTI-REFORMATION PRIEST, was eating dinner in a tavern in Cologne, Germany, where Peter Quentel was printing a book for him. A fireplace took the chill off the fall evening and the crowded tavern was a noisy place, but Cochlaeus could overhear a conversation between two of Quentel's printers.

After several steins of beer, when they were "in their cups," one printer mentioned a book they were printing that would sooner or later make Lutherans of everyone in England whether the king or cardinal liked it or not. Cochlaeus listened carefully.[III]

The second printer remarked that Quentel, their boss, was being very secretive about the project and would not let the printers talk to the British customers. The rumor was that they were very clever and that one even spoke eight languages.

Cochlaeus joined the two printers and invited them to his room. After serving several glasses of wine, he learned that they were printing three thousand copies of an English translation of the New Testament by William Tyndale. He also learned about plans to smuggle the books into England.

Cochlaeus went to the Cologne authorities, who investigated the matter, obtained an order to stop the printing, and wrote to King Henry VIII to watch the seaports "lest that pernicious article of merchandise should be conveyed into all parts of England." When Tyndale heard of the injunction, he did not wait to see what would happen next. He and his assistant, William

III Cochlaeus was no fan of vernacular translations of the Bible. He once wrote, "The New Testament translated into the vulgar tongue is in truth the food of death, the fuel of sin, the veil of malice, the pretext of false liberty, the protection of disobedience, the corruption of discipline, the depravity of morals, the termination of concord, the death of honesty, the wellspring of vices, the disease of virtues, the instigation of rebellion, the milk of pride, the nourishment of contempt, the death of peace, the destruction of charity, the enemy of unity, the murder of truth." (quoted by John Davidson, *The Gospel of Jesus* [Shaftesbury, UK: Element Books, Ltd., 1995, 2004], 70.)

In 1539 a royal proclamation said church officials should "expressly provoke, stir, and exhort every person to read" the Great Bible. It was received with such enthusiasm that officials put above this chained Great Bible in the crypt in St. Paul's in London an "Admonition" that parishioners should not disrupt church services by reading it too loudly. Sitting with her head on her hand and listening to John Porter's reading is Ann Askew, who had been turned out of her house by her husband for studying the Bible. She was later put on the rack so that she would tell authorities the names of those who studied Scriptures with her. The engraving is from a painting by Sir George Harvey.

Roy, gathered the manuscript and all the sheets that had already been printed and fled one hundred miles south to Worms.

No single person has had a more significant impact on the English Bible and no one has made a greater sacrifice than William Tyndale. He paid with his life—strangled while tied to a stake and then his body was burned.[112]

John Wycliffe had translated the Bible 150 years before Tyndale, but Wycliffe's Bible was written in Middle English and is as difficult to read today as Chaucer's *The Canterbury Tales*. Before Wycliffe and Chaucer, an Old English translation had been inserted between the lines of Latin in the Lindisfarne Gospels. And in 735 a godly monk named Bede, the Father of English History, translated the gospel of John into Old English at the end of his life.[113]

At the time of Tyndale the English language was still developing, and "what was once scorned as the barbarous language of plowmen, became esteemed as the language of patriots and poets. . . . To write in English (or to translate into English) was a political act, affirming the intrinsic dignity of the language of a newly confident people and nation."[114]

When William Tyndale was born near Wales in 1494, the *Constitutions* of 1408, which prohibited the reading of any nonapproved English Bible and had been enacted in response to Wycliffe's translation, were still actively enforced. Tyndale attended Oxford and then Cambridge. While serving as chaplain and tutor, Tyndale made his famous statement one evening in conversation at dinner with a clergyman: "I defy the pope, and all his laws," and added that if God spared his life, he would cause "a boy that drives the

112 At least Tyndale was not burned alive; that was a death reserved at the time for Anabaptists.

113 When Bede was almost finished with his translation, he was very weak. "Dear master," said his scribe, "there is still one chapter to do, but shouldn't you rest for a while?" "No, Be quick with your writing," Bede answered. "I cannot hold out much longer." The scribe wrote on. "And now, father, there is just one more sentence." Bede dictated it and said, "Write quickly." "It is finished, master." "Aye, it is finished!" echoed Bede and soon died while singing glory to God. (Miller, *General Biblical Introduction*, 320)

114 McGrath, *In the Beginning*, 24-25.

The Latin under William Tyndale's portrait says, "This picture represents . . . William Tyndale, sometime student of this hall [at Oxford University], . . . who, . . . devoted his energies to translating into the vernacular the New Testament and the Pentateuch, a labor so greatly tending to the salvation of his fellow countrymen that he was rightly called the Apostle of England. He gained a martyr's crown at Vilvorde near Brussels in 1536, a man, if we may believe even his adversary (the Emperor's Procurator General), learned, pious, and good." The picture hangs in the dining hall of Hertford College, Oxford.

plow to know more of the Scripture than" the clergyman himself did! Tyndale's words echoed those of Erasmus that the Bible should be available to "the farmer, the tailor, the mason, prostitutes, pimps, and Turk."

Tyndale sought approval from the bishop in London to make a new translation of the Bible. However, Henry VIII was still defender of the Catholic faith and permission was denied, and so Tyndale moved to Germany in 1524, never to return to England. In Germany he met Luther and, while living in Wittenberg, completed his translation of the New Testament. He began to have it printed in Cologne in a larger (quarto) size with notes in the margins. After he and William Roy fled to Worms, he had three—or perhaps six—thousand copies printed in a smaller (octavo) size without notes.

Early in 1526 copies of the New Testaments were smuggled into England "concealed in cases of merchandise, barrels, bales of cloth, sacks of flour and corn."[115] Henry opposed Tyndale's translation, and church officials bought copies to burn publicly. Opposition may have helped to increase circulation, and by the time of Tyndale's death more than fifty thousand copies of his New Testament had been sold in England (some of which, admittedly, had been burned). At one point a bishop visiting Europe negotiated through a merchant to buy all the copies Tyndale had of the New Testament so that he could take them back to England and burn them in London. A friend persuaded Tyndale that to do so would enable him to pay off his debts and provide enough money to print more copies with his latest corrections. "Forward went the bargain: the bishop had the books, Packingham [the merchant] had the thanks, and Tyndale had the money."[116] Tyndale next turned his attention to the Old Testament and published an English translation of the Pentateuch in 1530 and the book of Jonah in 1531.

British authorities would have liked to have Tyndale returned to England, and he spoke of "my pains . . . my poverty . . . my exile out of my natural country and bitter absence from my friends."[117] Tyndale wrote to Henry VIII that if the English text of the Bible were made freely available to Henry's subjects, Tyndale would return to England and submit to whatever pain, torture, or even death Henry might decide. Death was a very real possibility because, it is estimated, there were seventy-two thousand executions during Henry's 38-year reign.

In 1534, while living in the home of a British merchant in the Flemish port city of Antwerp in what is today Belgium, Tyndale published a thorough revision of the New Testament. This was also the year the British Parliament said it no longer recognized

115 Miller, *General Biblical Introduction*, 337.
116 Edward Hall, *The Union of the Two Noble and Illustre Families of Lancaster and York*, 1548.
117 Lightfoot, *How We Got the Bible*, 178.
118 Job 3:11; 13:19; 14:10.
119 Romans 13:1.
120 Genesis 4:9.
121 Matthew 5:13.
122 1 Timothy 6:12.
123 Romans 2:14.
124 A phrase used in a 1534 petition by the Convocation of Canterbury to Henry VIII. (McGrath, *In the Beginning*, 88).

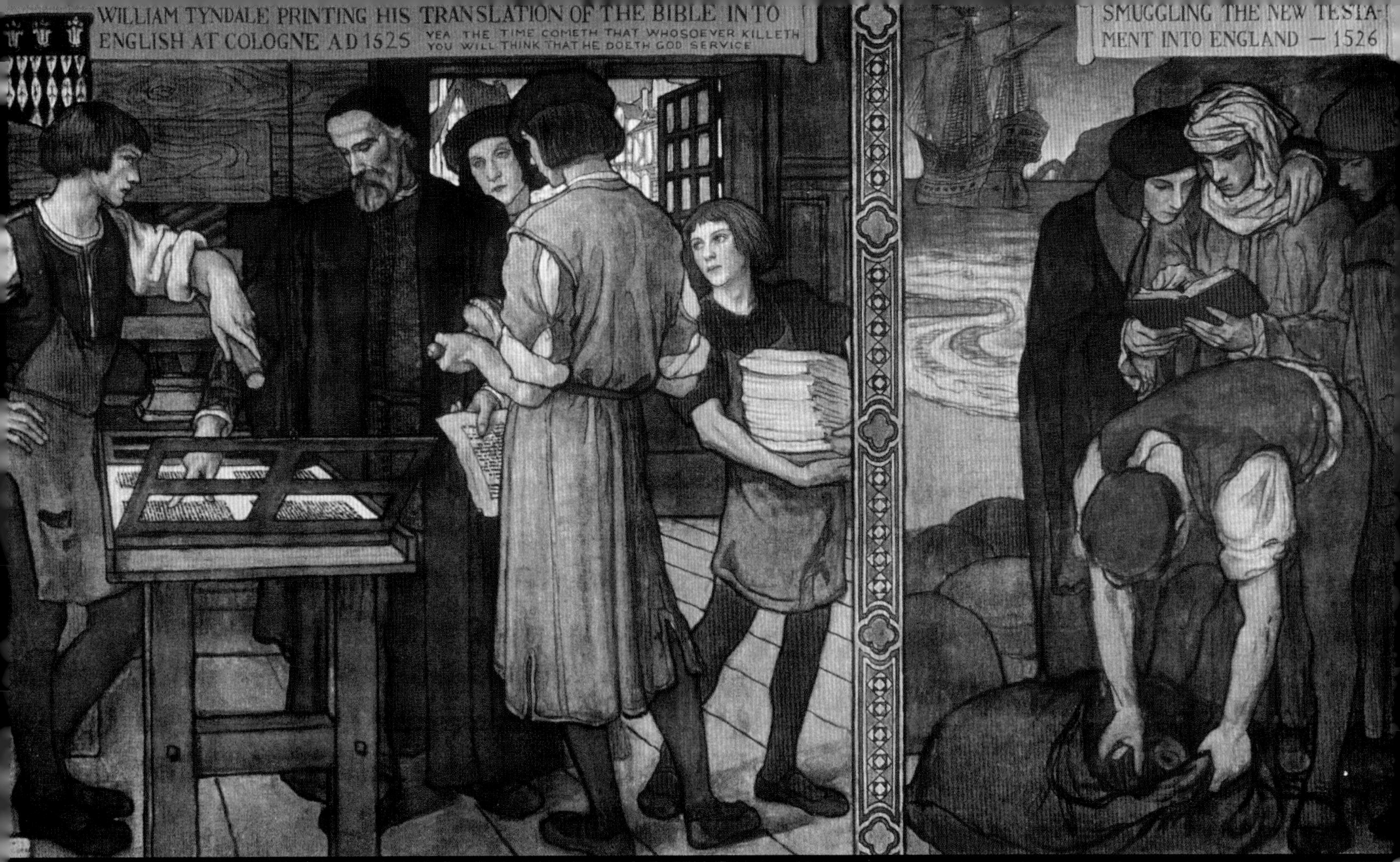
WILLIAM TYNDALE PRINTING HIS TRANSLATION OF THE BIBLE INTO ENGLISH AT COLOGNE AD 1525
YEA THE TIME COMETH THAT WHOSOEVER KILLETH YOU WILL THINK THAT HE DOETH GOD SERVICE
SMUGGLING THE NEW TESTAMENT INTO ENGLAND — 1526

William Tyndale began printing his translation of the New Testament at Peter Quentel's printing company in Cologne, Germany. When authorities ordered the printing stopped, Tyndale and his assistant fled to Worms where Peter Schoeffer finished printing the books. The New Testaments were smuggled into England "concealed in cases of merchandise, barrels, bales of cloth, sacks of flour and corn" and eagerly read. This mural by Violet Oakley is in the Pennsylvania State Capitol.

the supremacy of the pope, which should have helped Tyndale, but it did not. Antwerp was an island of tolerance in the midst of a cruel inquisition against Protestants, and in 1535 a young Englishman tricked Tyndale into going out of the house, and his enemies had him arrested. In spite of protests by the British government, Tyndale was in prison for sixteen months. "If I am to remain here through the winter," he wrote to the authorities, "have the kindness to send me . . . a warmer cap, . . . a warmer coat, . . . a piece of cloth too to patch my leggings. . . . But most of all . . . permit me to have the Hebrew Bible, Hebrew grammar, and Hebrew dictionary." Tyndale was tried and sentenced to death. His last words were a prayer: "Lord, open the King of England's eyes."

William Tyndale was a brilliant linguist and a superb translator. Many of the phrases in his translation are still in use today: "give up the ghost,"[118] "the powers that be,"[119] "my brother's keeper,"[120] "the salt of the earth,"[121] "fight the good fight,"[122] "a law unto themselves,"[123] and many more. Unlike Wycliffe, who translated portions of the Bible but was more an inspiration to others who did the work, Tyndale translated most of the Bible himself. In many respects the King James Version was a revision of Tyndale's translation.

Whether legal or illegal, the demand for Bibles in "the vulgar English tongue"[124] exploded, and over the next seventy-five years a number of significant translations were printed in England.

THE COVERDALE BIBLE (1535) - Tyndale died before completing his translation of the Old Testament. Miles Coverdale's translation was a complete English Bible. The second edition (1537) was done "with the King's most gracious license," meaning that people could read it freely and without fear of persecution.

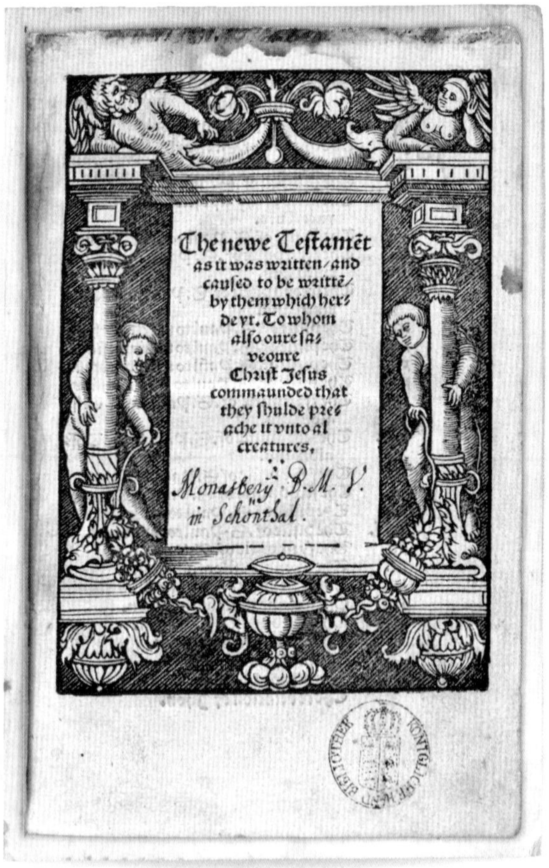
The newe Testamēt as it was written/and caused to be writtē/by them which herde yt. To whom also oure saveoure Christ Jesus commaunded that they shulde preache it vnto al creatures.

Monastery B.M.V. in Schontal.

Until the 1990s only two copies of the 1526 printing of Tyndale's New Testament, both incomplete and without title pages, were known to exist—one in St. Paul's Cathedral Library and one in the British Library that had been purchased from the Bristol Bible College. In November 1996, the only complete copy was discovered in the Württembergische Landesbibliothek in Stuttgart, Germany, a library with one of the world's most important collections of Bibles. The woodcut on the title page was used on many of the books printed by Peter Schoeffer in Worms; Tyndale would have chosen the words to be inserted in the central panel.

Coverdale made his translation not from Greek and Hebrew, but from Latin and German translations and compared it with Tyndale's. Coverdale's English is notable for being very readable.

THE MATTHEW'S BIBLE (1537) - Before William Tyndale died, he left his unfinished manuscript of the books of Joshua through II Chronicles with his friend, John Rogers, a Bible scholar who took the pseudonym of Thomas Matthew. The Matthew's Bible is a revision of Tyndale's New Testament with as much of the Old Testament as Tyndale had translated, supplemented by Coverdale's translation of the Old Testament books Tyndale did not translate. Rogers added marginal notes designed to help the "plowboy" understand the Scriptures, but he also left in some of Tyndale's notes and introductions that were critical of the Roman Catholic Church. In spite of those notes the Matthew's Bible received the "gracious license" of King Henry VIII, who, most likely, was not fully aware of what he was approving.

THE TAVERNER'S BIBLE (1539) - Richard Taverner, a Greek scholar and lawyer, was asked by a London printer to make some slight revisions in Matthew's Bible. There were only two printings, and it never had the chance to achieve popularity because of the royal approval given to The Great Bible.

THE GREAT BIBLE (1539) - England now had two Bibles "licensed" by the King. But the Coverdale Old Testament was not translated from Hebrew, and the Matthew's Bible had controversial notes in it by Tyndale and Rogers. Vicar-general Thomas Cromwell asked Coverdale to supervise another translation, a revision of Matthew's Bible. A royal proclamation said that a copy of the Great Bible should be placed in every church and that church officials should "expressly provoke, stir, and exhort every person to read" it. They did, and preachers reported that instead of listening to their sermons, some parishioners preferred to gather to read and discuss the Bible, sometimes in a disorderly fashion. Frederick Kenyon said, "The reading of the Bible took a firm hold on the people of England, a hold which has never since been relaxed, and which had much to do with the stable foundation of the Protestant church in this country."[125] Seven editions of The Great Bible were published between 1539 and 1541.

125 Frederic G. Kenyon, "English Versions," in *Dictionary of the Bible* ed. James Hastings (New York: Charles Scribner's Sons, 1909), reproduced on www.bible-researcher.com/greatbible1.html (accessed August 27, 2009). In the one hundred years since Kenyon made this statement, the hold of the Bible on the people of England has relaxed considerably.

126 This paragraph sounds as if it were written by a modern publisher's advertising copywriter, but it is all factual.

127 Harry Stout, "Word and Order in Colonial New England," in *The Bible in America*, ed. Nathan O. Hatch and Mark A. Noll, (Oxford: Oxford University Press, 1982), 21-22.

128 McGrath, *In the Beginning*, 129.

THE GENEVA BIBLE (1560) - Queen Mary I came to the throne in 1553 and tried to make Britain a Roman Catholic nation again through a reign of terror that included burning at the stake leading Protestants such as John Rogers, High Latimer, and Nicholas Ridley. At least eight hundred Protestants fled to Germany, Switzerland, and the independent city of Geneva, where several hundred waited for Mary's death. Those in Geneva decided there was a need for a new Bible translation. By the time the complete Bible was ready for publication in 1560, Mary had died and Elizabeth I, who wanted to be queen of "neither Papist nor Gospeller," was monarch, and so the Bible was dedicated to her.

Everything about the Geneva Bible made it accessible to the average person. It was available in small sizes and modest prices. Its typeface was easy to read and it introduced convenient verse divisions developed by Genevan printer Robert Stephanus. It was endorsed by such great reformers as John Knox, John Calvin (who wrote an introduction), and Theodore Beza. It contained five fold-out woodcut maps and extensive geographical, textual, and theological notes to explain "the hard places." [126] Because these Calvinistic notes were included in the Bible, they were widely circulated and tended to take on the authority of Scripture. "It would be difficult to overstate their influence in forming lay perceptions of godly living and Christian faith." [127] The Geneva Bible included the Apocrypha, but it was placed separately at the end of the Old Testament.

For more than fifty years the Geneva Bible was the Bible used by the common people of Britain and was printed in more than 160 editions. The Geneva Bible became part of England's Protestant national identity.[128] For Presbyterians and Puritans it became a symbol of all they wished to see reformed in the Church of England. It was the Bible Shakespeare read, the Bible Puritans carried with them to New England, and was widely used until 1616 when its printing was forbidden in England because of the King James Version.

In 1535 Tyndale was betrayed, arrested, and kept in prison for sixteen months in spite of the appeals of England's vicar-general, Thomas Cromwell. Tyndale was then tried for heresy and condemned to death. Led to the place of execution, he was tied to a stake and surrounded by kindling. His last words, spoken with fervent zeal and a loud voice, were "Lord, open the king of England's eyes." He was then strangled and his body burned. The woodcut is from Foxe's Book of Martyrs.

THE BISHOPS' BIBLE (1568) - When the Geneva Bible overtook the Great Bible in popularity among the common people, church authorities objected to its Calvinistic notes, and Archbishop Parker appointed a committee of bishops to revise the Great Bible, a revision called, appropriately, The Bishops' Bible. The revision was inconsistent in quality and sometimes stiff and formal. Queen Elizabeth did not endorse it, and although church authorities used it, ordinary people did not.

THE DOUAY-RHEIMS BIBLE (1582/1609-1610) - Just as Protestant scholars had fled England during Mary's reign and translated the Geneva Bible in exile, Catholic scholars left England during Elizabeth's

Henry VIII's desire for a male heir set into motion a series of events that led to the separation of the Church of England from Rome. Henry was named "Defender of the Faith" at first by Pope Leo X and then by the British parliament after the English church split from Rome. Although he did not approve Tyndale's work, Henry did not stop his subjects from reading the Coverdale Bible or the Matthew's Bible. In 1539, out of "his own liberty and goodness [Henry] was and is pleased that his said loving subjects should have and read"[129] *the Great Bible, which was to be placed in every church. This portrait shows a young Edward, who became king when he was only nine years old, Henry, and Jane Seymour, who actually died two weeks after giving birth to Edward. This painting from 1545 hangs at Hampton Court Palace.*

reign and translated an English Bible with Catholic notes and explanations. The translation was made from Latin, which, according to the introduction, is better "than the Greek text itself, in those places where they disagree" because it had been better preserved from corruption. The New Testament was published in 1582 and smuggled into England, but because of lack of funds, the complete Bible—named for the two cities in France where the exiles lived—was not published until twenty-seven years later. In 1738 London Bishop Richard Challoner did a major revision of Douay-Rheims, which became the standard English translation of the Bible for Roman Catholics until the mid-twentieth century.

We like to think that Bible translators and publishers are motivated by devotion to God and service to believers. In fact, politics and entrepreneurship play a major role as well. King James I of England had to deal with religious tensions between Anglicans, who believed in a close association of church and state, and Puritans, who wanted a church independent of the state. Because James had been king of Scotland, which was strongly Presbyterian, the English Puritans assumed he would be supportive of their calls for reform. However, James strongly believed in the "divine right of kings" and disliked the independence of the Presbyterians and Puritans, whom he called "pests," and their Geneva Bible.

Nevertheless, James called a conference at the Hampton Court Palace in January 1604 "for the reformation of some things amiss in ecclesiastical matters." Not much happened until John Reynolds, leader of the Puritan delegation, proposed a new Bible translation. James agreed immediately. "I confess," the king said, "I have never seen a Bible well translated, and the worst is the Geneva." He knew that a new English Bible, translated at his direction, would reinforce his image as political and spiritual leader of his people. He directed that the "best learned" in Cambridge and Oxford universities be appointed to do the translation, which would then be reviewed by bishops, then presented to the Privy Council, and finally to "be ratified by royal authority."

Like the Bishops' Bible, James's new translation was done by a committee. The king appointed 54 scholars, divided into six committees. Three were assigned to work on the Old Testament, two on the New Testament, and one on the Apocrypha. When

129 From a 1539 draft proclamation of Henry VIII's and quoted on a British Library podcast, http://britishlibrary.typepad.co.uk/henry/2009/07/new-podcast-henrys-great-bible.html (accessed Nov. 14, 2009).

130 Gordon Baker, "A Panoramic View of the King James Bible's Origins," *Anglican Journal*, (December 2003).

131 "The Holy Bible containing the Old Testament and the New. Newly translated out of the Originall tongues: & with the former Translations diligently compared and revised by his Majesties speciall Comandement. Appointed to bee read in Churches."

132 "Thou" is the subjective form (as is "I") and "thee" is the objective form (as is "me"), whereas the word "you" is both subjective and objective.

133 McGrath, *In the Beginning*, 266-7.

the committee work was finished, two members from each committee met for a final review of the entire Bible. After that, the bishops of Winchester and Gloucester reviewed the Bible, as did the archbishop of Canterbury. "There can be no question" that King James "and the bishops, scholars, and courtiers who surrounded him were all people of deep convictions, entrenched prejudices, flagrant ambitions, and committed to political 'hard ball.'"[130]

In spite of the claim of the title page that it was "newly translated,"[131] the committees did not start from scratch. Rather, they were specifically instructed to follow the Bishops' Bible as much as possible, and to follow "these translations . . . when they agree better with the Text than the Bishops' Bible: Tindoll's [Tyndale's], Matthew's, Coverdales's, Whitchurch's [The Great Bible], Geneva." The translators consulted the Greek (the Majority text of Erasmus) and Hebrew texts. In the preface they say they never set out to make a new translation, but to make "out of many good ones, one principal good one."

Because the translators were told to follow the Bishops' Bible, which followed the translation of the Great Bible (1539), which was a revision by Coverdale of Matthew's Bible (1537), which itself was a revision of Coverdale's first Bible (1535) that included Tyndale's translation, the King James Version includes much of the wording of Tyndale and Coverdale. This is demonstrated by the KJV's use of "thou" and "thee" instead of "you."[132] Alister McGrath says that "a careful study of the court records of the northern English city of Durham suggests that 'you' had replaced 'thou' as the normal form of address in spoken English by about 1575."[133]

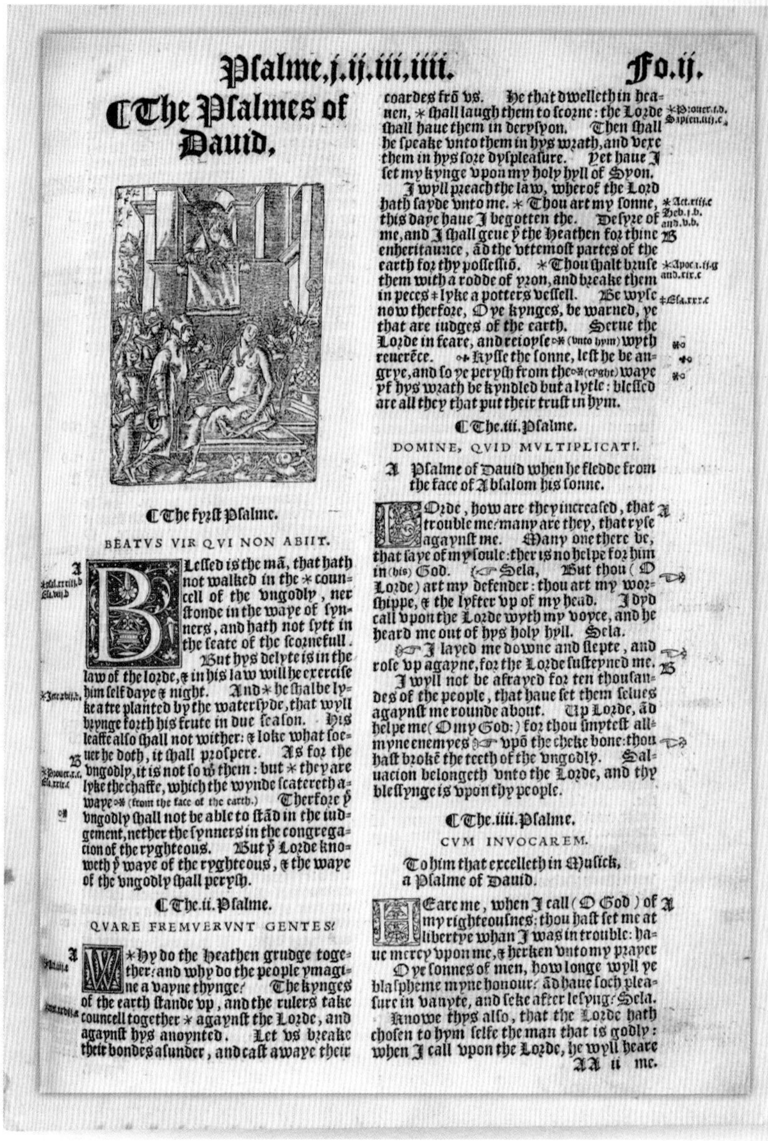

Psalme.i.ii.iii.iiii. Fo.ii.

¶ The Psalmes of Dauid.

¶ The fyrst Psalme.

BEATVS VIR QVI NON ABIIT.

A Blessed is the mã, that hath not walked in the * councell of the vngodly, ner stonde in the waye of synners, and hath not sytt in the seate of the scornefull. But hys delyte is in the law of the lorde, & in his law will he exercise him self daye & night. And * he shalbe lyke a tre planted by the watersyde, that wyll brynge forth his frute in due season. His leaffe also shall not wither: & loke what soeuer he doth, it shall prospere. B As for the vngodly, it is not so wt them: but * they are lyke the chaffe, which the wynde scatereth awaye (from the face of the earth.) Therfore y vngodly shall not be able to stãd in the iudgement, nether the synners in the congregacion of the ryghteous. But y Lorde knoweth y waye of the ryghteous, & the waye of the vngodly shall perysh.

¶ The.ii. Psalme.

QVARE FREMVERVNT GENTES?

A * Why do the heathen grudge together? and why do the people ymagine a vayne thynge? The kynges of the earth stande vp, and the rulers take councell together * agaynst the Lorde, and agaynst hys anoynted. Let vs breake their bondes asunder, and cast awaye their coardes frõ vs. He that dwelleth in heauen, * shall laugh them to scorne: the Lorde shall haue them in derysyon. Then shall he speake vnto them in hys wrath, and vexe them in hys sore dyspleasure. Yet haue I set my kynge vpon my holy hyll of Syon.

I wyll preach the law, wherof the Lord hath sayde vnto me. * Thou art my sonne, this daye haue I begotten the. Desyre of me, and I shall geue y the Heathen for thine B enheritaunce, ãd the vttemost partes of the earth for thy possessiõ. * Thou shalt bruse them with a rodde of yron, and breake them in peces ‡ lyke a potters vessell. Be wyse now therfore, O ye kynges, be warned, ye that are iudges of the earth. Serue the Lorde in feare, and reioyse (vnto hym) wyth reuerẽce. Kysse the sonne, lest he be angrye, and so ye perysh from the (ryght) waye yf hys wrath be kyndled but a lytle: blessed are all they that put their trust in hym.

¶ The.iii. Psalme.

DOMINE, QVID MVLTIPLICATI.

A Psalme of Dauid when he fledde from the face of Absalom his sonne.

A Lorde, how are they increased, that trouble me? many are they, that ryse agaynst me. Many one there be, that saye of my soule: ther is no helpe for him in (his) God. Sela. But thou (O Lorde) art my defender: thou art my worshippe, & the lyfter vp of my head. I dyd call vpon the Lorde wyth my voyce, and he heard me out of hys holy hyll. Sela.

I layed me downe and slepte, and rose vp agayne, for the Lorde susteyned me. B I wyll not be afrayed for ten thousandes of the people, that haue set them selues agaynst me rounde about. Up Lorde, ãd helpe me (O my God:) for thou smytest all myne enemyes vpõ the cheke bone: thou hast brokẽ the teeth of the vngodly. Saluacion belongeth vnto the Lorde, and thy blessynge is vpon thy people.

¶ The.iiii. Psalme.

CVM INVOCAREM.

To him that excelleth in Musick, a Psalme of Dauid.

A Heare me, when I call (O God) of my righteousnes: thou hast set me at libertye whan I was in trouble: haue mercy vpon me, & herken vnto my prayer

O ye sonnes of men, how longe wyll ye blasphemе myne honour? ãd haue soch pleasure in vanyte, and seke after lesyng? Sela. Knowe thys also, that the Lorde hath chosen to hym selfe the man that is godly: when I call vpon the Lorde, he wyll heare

AA ii me.

The Great Bible was the first English Bible authorized by the king. Its name comes from its size (10-3/8" x 15-1/8"). It was to be purchased by every parish and "set up in some convenient place" so that everyone could read it. The title page clearly sets out Henry's political agenda. He is pictured receiving the "Word of God" from God Himself, giving it to his ministers, who then give it to the people, all of whom are saying, "Long live the king." Henry is shown about four times the size of God. The page shown here is the beginning of Psalms.

When his mother, Mary, Queen of Scots, was imprisoned in 1567, thirteen-month old James VI became king of Scotland, where he ruled for thirty-five years. In 1603, he became James I, king of England, Scotland, and Ireland. The next year he directed the "best learned" in Cambridge and Oxford universities to create a new translation of the Bible, a translation that would reinforce his image as political and spiritual leader of his people and help achieve his goal of a unified Protestant England. His name is remembered in the designation of this best-loved of all English translations: the King James Version. Painting is by Paul van Somer.

thirty-five years before James's new translation. Genesis 3:11, in which God speaks to Adam, says in the KJV, "And he said, who told thee that thou wast naked? Hast thou eaten of the tree, whereof I commanded thee that thou shouldest not eat?" The Bishops' Bible, which the translators were supposed to follow, uses "thee" and "thou" but is more stilted: "And he sayde: Who tolde thee that thou wast naked? Hast thou not eaten of the same tree, concernyng the which I commaunded thee that thou shouldest not eate of it?" Evidently the translators went back to Coverdale's Bible: "And he sayde: who tolde the, that thou art naked? Hast thou not eaten of the tre, wherof I commaunded the, yt thou shuldest not eate."[134] The use of "thee" and "thou" in the KJV does not reflect spoken English in 1611. Instead it reflects spoken English in the early 1500s, one hundred years earlier.

When the six committees, twelve reviewers, two bishops, and one archbishop had finished their work, the manuscript was delivered to Robert Barker, who had a monopoly on printing Bibles in England.

The "new translation," as the King James Version was called, was published in 1611 with little fanfare. The first two printings were large (10-1/2" x 16") so that the Bible could be read in churches. Smaller editions were soon produced. Different printings varied in spelling, the illustrations used, the title page, and typographic errors. For instance, the word *not* was left out of the seventh commandment in "The Wicked Bible," which read, "Thou shalt commit adultery." If some sheets were left over from one printing, they were used in another. Almost no two existing "original 1611" Bibles are the same. Even today dealers have been known to piece together pages and sell them as a complete first edition.[135] Although the King James Version is today called the "Authorized Version," it was never given formal authorization by King James or anyone else.

Eventually the King James Version's prominence over the popular Geneva Bible had as much to do with its association with the monarchy and the Geneva Bible's association with the Puritans as with quality of translation or cost of the Bibles. In 1616 the printing of the Geneva Bible was forbidden in

134 Tyndale's translation says, "And he said: who told the that thou wast naked? Hast thou eaten of the tree, of which I bade the that thou shouldest not eate?"

135 Donald Brake mentions Francis Fry, a nineteenth-century scholar who "believed he understood which signatures and reprinted leaves belonged to the first and second issues [of the KJV]. Over the course of many years, he gathered copies and exchanged leaves according to his theory. . . . Fry is not the only one to be blamed for this reprehensible practice. . . . Today people put together various copies of the folio editions and call them *editio princeps* in order to sell them as first editions of 1611." (*A Visual History of the English Bible*, 201).

136 Frederic W. Farrar, *The Bible: Its Meaning and Supremacy* (London: Longmans, Green, & Co., 1901), 260.

England, but copies were simply printed in Netherlands and imported. When the Puritan Parliament in London fell apart and the English monarchy was restored in 1660, the demand for the Geneva Bible seemed to evaporate and the King James Version achieved dominance.

There were various calls for corrections and revisions to the King James Version because of printers' errors in the early editions and changes in spelling and word usage over the years. The most significant correction was in 1762—150 years after the KJV was first published—by F. S. Paris. The work of Dr. Paris was refined by Benjamin Blayney in 1769, which then became the standard King James Version used until today.

THE KING JAMES VERSION . . . HAS HELPED FORM OUR language, has given context to our literature, has inspired our music, and for centuries it was the one book a family would own and read before all others.

The copyright status of the KJV is unique. In most of the world it is no longer under copyright protection. In the United Kingdom, however, the copyright is held by the British Crown and can be printed only by license from the king or queen.

Hampton Court Palace, southwest of central London, is a magnificent palace of Henry VIII's that was later expanded by other monarchs. In 1604, less than a year after becoming King of Great Britain, James I called a conference with "bishops and other learned men" of the Church of England and four moderate Puritans. When Puritan John Reynolds proposed a new Bible translation, James agreed immediately and the King James Version was born.

THE INFLUENCE OF THE KING JAMES VERSION on English civilization has been profound. It has helped form our language; it has given context to our literature; it has inspired our music; and for centuries it was the one book a family would own and read before all others. The experience of British art critic John Ruskin was not unusual: "Whatever greatness there has been in any thought of mine . . . has simply been due to the fact that, when I was a child, my mother daily read with me a part of the Bible, and daily made me learn a part of it by heart."[136] Victor Hugo, author of *Les Miserables*, said, "England has two books, the Bible and Shakespeare. England made Shakespeare, but the Bible made England."

Wherever the British went, they took the King James Bible with them. The first English Bible printed in the New World was a King James Version, and its words can be found in American place names,

On November 5, 1605, the evening before Parliament opened, a soldier named Guy Fawkes was discovered in the cellar of the Parliament building guarding a pile of wood and thirty-six barrels of gunpowder. A part of a Catholic conspiracy led by Robert Catesby, his intention was to blow up the House of Lords the next day and cause the destruction, as King James put it, "not only...of my person, nor of my wife and posterity also, but of the whole body of the State in general" and reestablish Catholicism in England. This is a contemporary picture of eight of the thirteen conspirators, who were tried and executed.

political speeches, and literature. It was the foundation of early education. On its three hundredth anniversary, Theodore Roosevelt said that the KJV Bible is "the Magna Carta of the poor and the oppressed . . . the most democratic book in the world." British missionaries took the King James Version from the outback of Australia to Chief Chitambo's village in Zambia.[137]

Around the world people have been comforted by the words, "The Lord is my shepherd, I shall not want"[138] and "Come unto me, all ye that labour and are heavy laden, and I will give you rest."[139] They have been challenged by the words, "Judge not, that ye be not judged"[140] and "Be strong and of a good courage; be not afraid, neither be thou dismayed: for the Lord thy God is with thee whithersoever thou goest."[141] They have celebrated with the words, "Fear not: for, behold, I bring you good tidings of great joy, which shall be to all people. For unto you is born this day in the city of David a Saviour, which is Christ the Lord."[142] And the words of the King James Version have expressed the heart of the Christian message with a poetic beauty: "But now is Christ risen from the dead. . . . For as in Adam all die, even so in Christ shall all be made alive."[143]

The King James Version has been treasured for four hundred years. "Wherever in the world there are English readers, there are copies. In the story of the earth we live on, its influence cannot be calculated. Its words have been found to have a unique quality, of being able both to lift up a dedicated soul higher than had been thought, and to reach even below the lowest depths of human experience. . . . Sometimes the translation is wrong, or clumsy, or baffling. KJV's readings of the base texts are in hundreds of places now superseded by greater knowledge, or just better texts. Its older English can confuse the tongue. In particulars, it is not perfect. But the great love it has received is justified by its master of the craft of the declaration of an incarnate God."[144]

137 David Livingstone, pioneer missionary to Africa, died in Chief Chitambo's village in 1873. Livingstone's body was carried back to London and is buried in Westminster Abbey. His heart, however, is buried in Africa.
138 Psalm 23:1.
139 Matthew 11:28.
140 Matthew 7:1.
141 Joshua 1:9.
142 Luke 2:10-11.
143 1 Corinthians 15:20, 22.
144 David Daniell, *The Bible in English: Its History and Influence* (New Haven, Connecticut: Yale University Press, 2003), 427-28.

YOU CAN'T TELL THE PLAYERS WITHOUT A PROGRAM

OR, MORE THAN YOU REALLY WANT TO KNOW ABOUT THE BRITISH MONARCHY

Christianity arrived in Britain sometime before the third century. The pope sent missionaries to Britain in the sixth century, and for more than one thousand years most of the Christian church in Britain was under papal authority. When the Reformation exploded in Europe, Britain was still a Catholic nation. In 1521 Pope Leo X named King Henry VIII "Defender of the Faith" for a book he wrote defending, ironically, the sacramental nature of marriage and papal supremacy.

Britain's loyalty to the pope changed, however, when, in order to produce a male heir, Henry wanted Pope Clement VII to annul his marriage to Catherine of Aragon so he could marry Anne Boleyn. The pope refused, Henry separated the Church of England from the Church in Rome in 1534, became the head of the English Church, and had his marriage annulled. Pope Paul III then excommunicated Henry. Several years later the British parliament declared that Henry's son, Edward VI, was "Defender of the Faith," a title that is still held by British monarchs, indicating that they are head of the Anglican Church.

Henry VIII's quarrel with the Roman Catholic Church was not theological, and so he never embraced the teachings of the Reformation, even though the Church of England separated from Rome. He did, however, acquire all the monastic lands and the church's assets in Britain. At the end of his life Henry became grossly overweight, irritable, harsh, and tyrannical. He died in 1547 and was followed by his nine-year-old son, Edward VI, who encouraged Protestants. Edward died six years later when he was only fifteen and was followed by Mary, who made Britain Catholic again. Those who did not cooperate were burned at the stake for heresy, earning her the nickname "Bloody Mary." When Mary died in 1558, she was followed by her half sister, Elizabeth I, who was Protestant but was tolerant of Catholics. The Spanish tried to conquer Britain in 1588, during Elizabeth's reign, and make it a Catholic nation again, but the spectacular failure of the Spanish Armada solidified England as a Protestant nation.

There was no clear successor to Elizabeth I. Henry VIII had made careful provision for succession after his death, but none of his children had produced any children. The next monarch would therefore be a descendant of Henry VIII's father, Henry VII. Henry VII's oldest daughter had married James IV of Scotland and their great grandson, James VI, became king of Scotland at one year of age when his mother, Mary, Queen of Scots, was imprisoned. In 1603 James VI of Scotland became James I of Great Britain (England, Scotland, Wales) and Ireland.

Certain Catholics again attempted to make England a Catholic nation by force, but, like the attempt by the Spanish Armada, they failed. They put thirty-six barrels containing more than one and a half tons of gunpowder in a room immediately under the House of Lords, intending to blow it up when parliament opened on November 5, 1605, with King James in attendance. The plot was discovered, the conspirators tried and executed, and the Protestant toleration of Catholics put back for centuries.

HOUSE OF TUDOR AND HOUSE OF STUART

MONARCH	REIGN	FAITH	RELATIONSHIP
	House of Tudor		
Henry VII	1485–1509	Catholic	son of Edmund Tudor and Lady Margaret Beaufort
Henry VIII	1509–1547	Catholic/ Protestant	son of Henry VII
Edward VI	1547–1553	Protestant	son of Henry VIII and Jane Seymour
Lady Jane Gray	nine days in 1553	Protestant	great-granddaughter of Henry VII; grandniece of Henry VIII
Mary I	1553–1558	Catholic	daughter of Henry VIII and Catherine of Aragon
Elizabeth I	1558–1603	Protestant	daughter of Henry VIII and Anne Boleyn
	House of Stuart (Scottish)		
James I	1603–1625	Protestant	great-great-grandson of Henry VII; as son of Mary, Queen of Scots, he was also King James VI of Scotland
Charles I	1625–1649	Protestant	son of James I
	No monarch from 1649–1660		
Charles II	1660–1685	Protestant	son of Charles I
James II	1685–1688	Catholic	son of Charles I; brother of Charles II
William III*	1689–1702	Protestant	grandson (through his mother) of Charles I; husband of Mary II
Mary II*	1689–1694	Protestant	daughter of James II
Anne	1702–1714	Protestant	daughter of James II; sister of Mary II

*William III and Mary II, husband and wife, were joint sovereigns with equal powers. After Mary's death in 1694, William reigned alone. They were childless.

The Lord to mee a shepheard is,
want therefore shall not I.
Hee in the folds of tender-grasse,
doth cause mee downe to lie.
(Psalm 23:1-2, *The Bay Psalm Book*)

8

THE OLD BOOK IN THE NEW WORLD

THE FIRST BOOK PRINTED IN AMERICA WAS A PSALTER— the psalms written in meter by "thirty pious and learned Ministers."

The Massachusetts Bay Colony was not the first settlement in America. Jamestown was established by the British in 1607, the Dutch settled on Manhattan Island in 1613, and the Pilgrims landed in Plymouth in 1620. But with nearly half the people of European descent in America living in the Massachusetts Bay Colony, it was by far the largest. A printing press was brought to Cambridge specifically to print the Psalter, and in 1640 Stephen Daye printed seventeen hundred copies of *The Bay Psalm Book*. It went through several editions and its words were sung in churches for one hundred years.

It was appropriate that the first book printed in America was a Psalter because America was founded on the Bible. The first colonists in New England came for freedom to worship the God of the Bible. The first colleges were founded to educate ministers to teach the Bible.[145] In 1777 a committee of the Continental Congress pointed out that "the use of the Bible is so universal and its importance so great" that Congress should import twenty thousand Bibles.[146] America became a nation filled with biblical images, biblical language, and biblical teaching. The Bible has been a book central to the faith of many Americans—and

145 One of Harvard's "College Laws" from 1642 to 1650 was "Every one shall so exercise himself in reading the Scriptures twice a day that they bee ready to give an account of their proficiency therein" (S.E. Morrison, *The Founding of Harvard College* [Cambridge, Massachusetts: Harvard University Press, 1935], 333-334).

146 From a report by a committee of the Continental Congress (John Wright, *Early Bibles of America* [New York: Thomas Whittaker, 1894] quoted in P. Marion Simms, *The Bible in America*, [New York: Wilson-Erickson, 1936], 126).

America was founded on the Bible. In 1837 the U.S. Congress commissioned Robert Weir to paint The Embarkation of the Pilgrims from Delft-Haven, in Holland *for one of the four then remaining niches in the Capitol rotunda. This romantic painting reflects America's image of itself in the mid-nineteenth century. The Pilgrims' pastor, John Robinson, boarded the Speedwell to lead the families in prayer while William Brewster, in the center of the painting, holds a Bible opened to the beginning of the New Testament. A rainbow at the left symbolizes hope and divine protection.*

that's one story. For others "the Bible was not so much the truth above all truth as it was the story above all stories,"[147] a part of their cultural heritage—and that's another story. Both stories are important when talking about the Bible in America.

The first settlers in New England came seeking religious freedom. The Pilgrims, who were Puritans wanting to separate from the Church of England, brought the Geneva Bible with them in 1620 and established a colony "for the Glory of God, and Advancement of the Christian Faith."[148] The Massachusetts Bay Colony was founded by nonseparating Puritans so that the example of peaceful and civil government and "orderlie Conversation maie wynn and incite the Natives of Country to the Knowledg and Obedience of the onlie true God and Savior of Mankinde, and the Christian Fayth."[149] When the governments of Massachusetts, Connecticut, New Plymouth, and New Haven organized the New England Confederation in 1643, they stated, "We all came into these parts of America with one and the same end and aim, namely, to advance the Kingdom of our Lord Jesus Christ and to enjoy the liberties of the Gospel in purity with peace."[150] These kinds of statements are in many of the founding documents of America's colonies.

Certainly many of those coming to America were motivated by reasons other than their religious faith. Most of the settlers in Jamestown were seeking opportunity and wealth. Within a couple of years of the Pilgrims' arrival, a settlement was established nearby filled with "rude and profane fellows." Some settlers were convicts transported across the Atlantic from English prisons. Others came for adventure. And those colonists who wanted religious freedom for themselves did not necessarily want it for others. The 1609 charter of the Virginia Company stated that

147 Mark Noll, "The Image of the United States as a Biblical Nation, 1776–1865," in Nathan O. Hatch and Mark A. Noll, eds. *The Bible in America* (New York: Oxford University Press, 1982), 43.
148 The Mayflower Compact, November 11, 1620.
149 The Charter of Massachusetts Bay, March 4, 1629.
150 The Articles of Confederation of the United Colonies of New England, May 19, 1643.

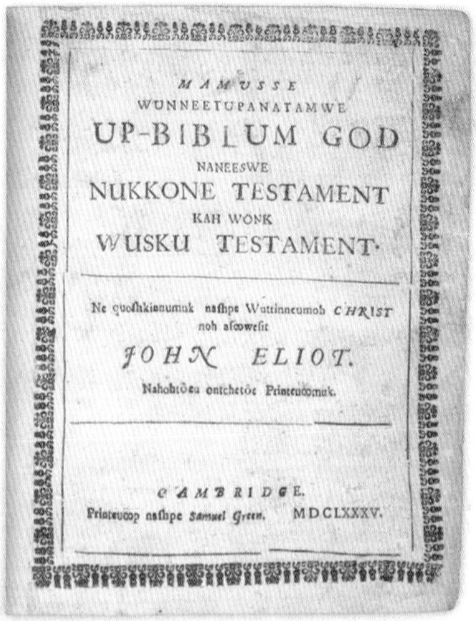

MAMUSSE
WUNNEETUPANATAMWE
UP-BIBLUM GOD
NANEESWE
NUKKONE TESTAMENT
KAH WONK
WUSKU TESTAMENT.

Ne quoshkinnumuk nashpe Wuttinneumoh CHRIST
noh asoowesit
JOHN ELIOT.
Nahohtôeu ontchetôe Printeuoomuk.

CAMBRIDGE.
Printeuoop nashpe Samuel Green. MDCLXXXV.

Puritan pastor John Eliot arrived in Massachusetts Bay Colony in 1631. Fifteen years later he had learned the Natick dialect of Algonquin, well enough to preach sermons in it (above). His dedication to the Algonquin and his love for them led him to be called "the apostle to the Indians." Eliot's translation of the New Testament (1661) and then the complete Bible (1663) was the first Bible printed in America. This title page (right) is from a second printing that was made in 1685 after many copies of the first printing were destroyed in a war against the British by a Wampanoag chief known as King Philip.

there could be no settlers who "we suspected to affect the Superstitions of the Church of Rome."[151] This charter was given by James I just four years after Guy Fawkes and Catholic conspirators had tried to blow up the parliament building and assassinate the king, so it is understandable that James did not feel kindly toward Catholics. In 1636 Roger Williams founded Rhode Island because he wanted religious freedom, but it was religious freedom from the authorities in Massachusetts who felt that Williams's sermons stating that the Church of England was apostate and the King of England was not a Christian were too extreme.

The first Bible printed in America was a translation into the Natick dialect of Algonquin, one of the world's most difficult languages, made by John Eliot, who took time from his church in Roxbury, Massachusetts, to visit the Indians. "The weather was cold and snowy. Was wet for the entire time but that is a small price to pay for the privilege of taking the Gospel to them,"[152] he wrote. Eliot gathered eleven hundred "praying Indians" into fourteen self-governing communities and spent ten years translating the Bible. The New Testament was printed in 1661 and the complete Bible in 1663. A second printing was made after many of the Bibles were destroyed in 1675 in a war against the British by a Wampanoag chief known as King Philip.

The first Bible printed in a European language in America was Martin Luther's German translation. Christopher Saur, a creative and energetic immigrant in Germantown, now a part of Philadelphia, was a printer of a German newspaper and almanac. His crowning achievement was a Bible printed in 1743. His son made a second printing in 1763 after his father's death. In 1776 sheets for a third printing were ready for the binder when soldiers invaded Germantown and used the pages as bedding for their horses and to make cartridges for their guns.

America became a patchwork of Christian groups, reflecting the denominations and nationalities that had come to the New World. Massachusetts, where only church members could vote, became Congregational, and Virginia was Anglican. Rhode Island, the birthplace of the Baptists in America, was founded on the principle of freedom of conscience. When Quakers learned they were not welcome in

151 The Second Charter of Virginia, May 23, 1609.
152 Herbert Samworth, "John Eliot and America's First Bible, http://www.solagroup.org/articles/historyofthebible/hotb_0005.html (accessed August 27, 2009).
153 Quoted in Harry S. Stout, "Word and Order in Colonial New England," in Hatch and Noll, eds. *The Bible in America*, 34.
154 This phrase is attributed to G. K. Chesterton (Sidney E. Mead, "The 'Nation with the Soul of a Church,'" in Russell E. Richey and Donald G. Jones, *American Civil Religion* [New York: Harper & Row, 1974] 45).

New England, they moved to Pennsylvania and founded a "holy experiment" where the oppressed of any belief could find refuge. In 1683 German Mennonites settled at Germantown and later Moravians established a community in Bethlehem.

Between 1725 and 1760 these denominational distinctions began to blur when a series of revivals swept across the colonies and a common conversion experience led to a more common understanding of the Christian faith. The First Great Awakening resulted in countless conversions, called believers to a life of piety and Bible study, motivated missionaries, created colleges such as Princeton, Rutgers, and Brown, and increased aid to the poor.

When delegates to the Continental Congress gathered in Philadelphia in 1774 and 1775, therefore, they represented people who had just seen a tremendous religious awakening and held the Bible in high esteem. Although the Enlightenment taught that human reason was the primary source of authority, preachers such as Jonathan Edwards and George Whitfield emphasized the divine authority of the Bible.

When the thirteen colonies declared their independence from England and became a new nation, stories and images were chosen to define the new country—and many were biblical. America was seen as a promised land. God had singled out Americans like the Israelites of the Old Testament to bless the people of the earth. In 1630 John Winthrop, governor of Massachusetts Bay Colony, alluded to Christ's words in the Sermon on the Mount when he said that America "shall be as a city upon a hill. The eyes of all people are upon us." These words were later used by presidents John F. Kennedy and Ronald Reagan to describe America. In a sermon preached to the legislators of the Massachusetts Bay Colony in 1776, Congregational Minister Samuel West said, "I cannot help hoping, and even believing, that Providence has designed this continent for to be the asylum of liberty and true religion."[153] America became "a nation with the soul of a church."[154]

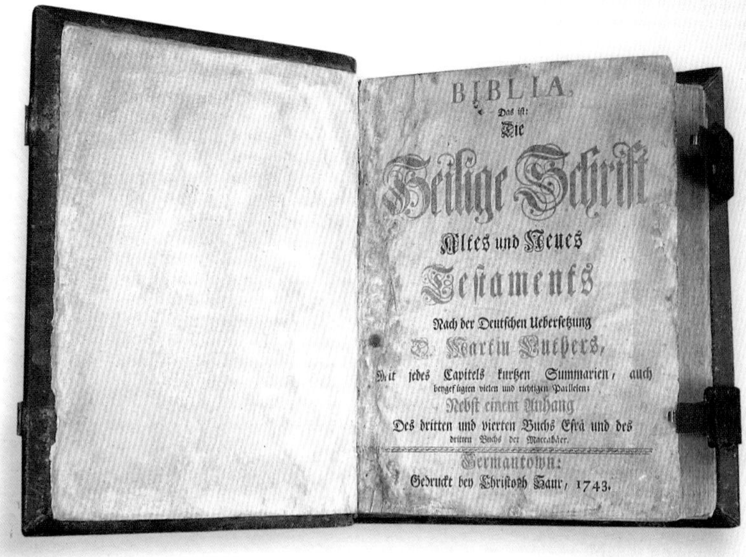

The first printing of a Bible in a European language in the New World was twelve hundred copies of Martin Luther's German translation in 1743 by Christopher Sauer. Sauer wanted to help Germans in the colonies preserve their ethnic culture, and so he published a German-language newspaper, an almanac, and books. But his crowning achievement was the Bible. For more than twenty-five years the Germantown congregation of Brethren met in his home. His son made a second printing of the Bible in 1763 and a third in 1776, although nearly all the copies of the third printing were destroyed by soldiers.

Not everyone agreed. Thomas Jefferson was opposed to denominational dogma and pasted together a story of Jesus without any miracles by literally cutting parts out of a printed Bible and pasting them in a "wee little book" of forty-six pages. Thomas Paine was more outspoken. In *The Age of Reason*, an irreverent book he wrote in France, Paine said of the Old Testament, "the obscene stories, the voluptuous debaucheries, the cruel and torturous executions, the unrelenting vindictiveness with which more than half the Bible is filled . . . is a history of wickedness that has served to corrupt and brutalize mankind." When he died, *The New York Citizen* said that Thomas Paine "had lived long, did some good and much harm."

Jefferson and Paine notwithstanding, America's common language and common heritage was the Bible. Many towns had biblical names.

Between 1725 and 1750 a series of revivals, called the First Great Awakening, swept across the colonies so that when the delegates to the Continental Congress gathered, they represented people who held the Bible in high esteem. In September 1774, its chaplain, Jacob Duché, read Psalm 35 and opened the First Continental Congress with a prayer that God "look down in mercy . . . on these our American States" and that "truth and justice, religion and piety, prevail and flourish amongst the people." John Adams said that the prayer had a profound effect on the delegates.

Biblical allusions permeated American literature. Benjamin Franklin and a Congressional committee proposed that the national seal picture Moses leading Israel through the Red Sea, a reference to America's freedom from Britain.

African-Americans identified with the same biblical story, but with a very literal cry, along with Moses, to "let my people go." Those slave owners who read the Bible themselves would usually read it to their house slaves. Some whites even taught blacks to read so that they could read the Bible,[155] but many preferred that their slaves remain illiterate. When the Bible was read to slaves, it would include passages such as "Servants, obey in all things your masters."[156] When slaves read the Bible for themselves, they discovered it also included "Masters, give unto your servants that which is just and equal."[157] As African-Americans encountered the stories of the Bible, they made the stories their own and retold them through Negro spirituals.

Later the Bible gave African-Americans the resources and words to critique injustice. "From W.E.B. DuBois to Toni Morrison, black writers have invoked Jesus to signify the suffering of black people."[158] The Bible gave hope to slaves and to free blacks, not just of a better life in heaven but also here on earth. It was biblical imagery that defined the dreams that their children "would not be judged by the color of their skin but by the content of their character" and that one day "every valley shall be exalted, every hill and mountain shall be made low, the rough places will be made plain, and the crooked places will be made straight, and the glory of the Lord shall be revealed, and all flesh shall see it together."[159]

ALTHOUGH THE FIRST BOOK PRINTED IN AMERICA was *The Bay Psalm Book*, the colonists could not print the King James Version as long as they were subject to British law because that right was limited to printers licensed by the crown. Moreover, Bibles could be printed more easily and cheaply in England and exported to America. When the colonies declared their independence in 1776, the British restricted the exportation of Bibles and other books to America and Congress solicited bids from printers. Learning that printing Bibles was too expensive, it was then recommended that Congress import twenty thousand Bibles "from Holland, Scotland, or elsewhere." But because of the British army's capture of Philadelphia and lack of money, the Bibles were never imported.

Robert Aitken, one of the five Philadelphia printers who had given a bid, printed a New Testament in 1777, and encouraged by his success asked for the financial support of Congress to print the entire Bible. The money was never granted, but Aitken printed ten thousand copies of the complete Bible anyway in 1782, the first English Bible printed in America. In the

155 One notable example is the Confederate General Stonewall Jackson. While he was a professor at Virginia Military Institute and deacon at Lexington's Presbyterian Church, Jackson taught Sunday school to slaves and free blacks. Hundreds of children were taught to read by one of the greatest generals in American history.

156 Colossians 3:22 (KJV).

157 Colossians 4:1 (KJV).

158 Review of Allen Dwight Callahan, *The Talking Book: African Americans and the Bible* (New Haven, Connecticut: Yale University Press, 2006) in *Publisher's Weekly*, August 18, 2006.

159 Martin Luther King, in a speech on August 28, 1963, on the steps of the Lincoln Memorial, referring to Isaiah 40:4.

160 Quoted in Garry Wills, "Mason Weems, Bibliopolist," *American Heritage* (February-March, 1981), 68.

front he reproduced a resolution passed by the Continental Congress on September 10, 1782:

> The United States in Congress assembled highly approve the pious and laudable undertaking of Mr. Aitken, . . . and . . . recommend this edition of the Bible to the inhabitants of the United States, and hereby authorize him to publish this recommendation in the manner he shall think proper.

AMERICA'S COMMON LANGUAGE AND . . . HERITAGE WAS THE BIBLE. Many towns had biblical names. . . . Benjamin Franklin . . . proposed that the national seal picture Moses leading Israel through the Red Sea.

TODAY FEWER THAN FORTY COPIES OF AITKEN'S Bible exist, making it one of the rarest books in the world. While the Bibles were being printed the colonies were at war with England, and at one point Aitken had to bury the type in a barn to prevent British soldiers from destroying it. Seven years later Aitken asked Congress to grant him the exclusive right to print Bibles in America for fourteen years. The request was denied, and by 1800 there were fifteen editions of the New Testament and twenty of the whole Bible in print from a variety of American printers.

Matthew Carey, an Irish-Catholic printer, set up shop in Philadelphia, and in 1790 he printed America's first English Catholic Bible, the Douay-Rheims Version. It was not financially successful, but his printings of the King James Version, beginning in 1801, were very profitable. Pioneering the mass production and distribution of Bibles, Carey competed in price, with a variety of bindings, and with the most "curious, usurious and wonderful" editions available. Mason Weems, a traveling salesman for Carey, wrote, "I tell you this is the very season and age of the Bible. Bible Dictionaries, Bible tales, Bible stories—Bibles plain or paraphrased, Carey's Bibles, Collin's Bibles, Clarke's Bibles, Kimptor's Bibles, no matter what or whose, all, all will go down—so wide is the crater of public appetite at this time."[160]

Carey's business was helped by the Second Great Awakening, which began about 1790, lasted for fifty years, and led to prison reform, temperance, women's suffrage, and the abolitionist movement. Central and western New York State was so filled with revivals in the first half of the nineteenth century that many religious movements started there, most notably Seventh-Day Adventism and Mormonism. It almost looked as if the Roman Catholic argument made during the Reformation that left to the judgement of individuals, the Bible could be subjected to a thousand viewpoints and Christianity divided into a thousand sects would come true in the United States.

The Bible gave African Americans the resources and words to critique injustice. On August 28, 1963, for instance, Rev. Martin Luther King, speaking from the steps of the Lincoln Memorial, said, referring to Isaiah 40:4, "I have a dream that one day every valley shall be exalted, every hill and mountain shall be made low, the rough places will be made plain, and the crooked places will be made straight, and the glory of the Lord shall be revealed, and all flesh shall see it together. . . . With this faith, we will be able to hew out of the mountain of despair a stone of hope. With this faith, we will be able to transform the jangling discords of our nation into a beautiful symphony of brotherhood."

THE CHICAGO TRIBUNE.

Revised New Testament Edition.

SUNDAY MAY 22, 1881—SIXTEEN PAGES.

THE

NEW TESTAMENT

OF OUR LORD AND SAVIOR

JESUS CHRIST,

TRANSLATED OUT OF THE GREEK:

Being the Version Set Forth A. D. 1611, Compared with the Most Ancient Authorities and Revised A. D. 1881.

PRINTED FOR CHICAGO AND THE NORTHWEST.

CHICAGO:
THE CHICAGO TRIBUNE PRESS.

THE GOSPELS.

ST. MATTHEW.

The longest telegram ever sent was 118,000 words of the Revised Version telegraphed from New York to Chicago so that the complete New Testament could be printed in the May 22, 1881, edition of The Chicago Tribune *and* The Chicago Times. *After receiving the telegram, ninety-two compositors worked twelve hours to set the New Testament in type.*

The American Bible Society was founded in 1816 and four times in the nineteenth century it conducted campaigns to give a Bible to every family in the United States that did not already have one. Between 1882 and 1890 more than six million families were visited and nearly half a million received a Bible.

THE KING JAMES VERSION WAS THE BIBLE READ BY the American colonists after 1700, that preachers used in both Great Awakenings, and from which soldiers on both sides in the Civil War received comfort. Although the King James Version had been revised in the 1760s in England, the first major revision did not occur until the 1870s, when the language was updated and changes were made based on the latest discoveries in Greek manuscripts, specifically the Westcott and Hort Greek text.

There had been a few Bible translations in the nineteenth century, but none of lasting importance. Noah Webster made his own revision of the King James Version in 1833 for use in schools. He made sure that grammar was correct, words understandable, and removed expressions that were "so offensive, especially to females, as to create a reluctance in young persons to attend Bible classes and schools, in which they are required to read passages which cannot be repeated without a blush." The story of the Bible in the United States from 1881 to today is largely the story of the many translations of the Bible into English.

The REVISED VERSION (RV) of the New Testament was published in May 1881 to an overwhelmingly enthusiastic reception. Three million copies were sold in the first year. Matthew through Romans (about 118,000 words) was telegraphed from New York to Chicago so that the entire New Testament could be quickly reproduced in the *Chicago Tribune* and *Chicago Times*. Some of the translation's policies—such as always translating a Greek word with the same English word—made for stilted reading. "Strong in Greek, weak in English," said British preacher Charles Spurgeon. The Old Testament was published in 1885.

An American committee had consulted with the English revisers and in 1901 it published the AMERICAN STANDARD VERSION (ASV). The ASV received a more permanent reception in America than the English version did in Britain, but neither displaced the beloved King James Version.

In 1929 the World Council of Churches decided that a new translation was needed. The REVISED STANDARD VERSION (RSV) New Testament was published in 1946 and the complete Bible in 1952 with funding from Thomas Nelson & Sons, which received a ten-year exclusive right to publish the translation. Although the RSV was controversial (fundamental and evangelical Protestants preferred the KJV, and liberal Protestants used the RSV), it was the first translation to challenge the popularity of the King James Version. It also launched a flood of Bible translations that has not stopped. A NEW REVISED STANDARD VERSION (NRSV) with gender-neutral language was published in 1989.

The NEW ENGLISH BIBLE (NEB) (1961, 1970) was the work of British and European scholars

When the Revised Standard Version Bible was published in 1952, one and a half million people participated in 3,500 community observances. Here, Luther Weigle, chairman of the translation committee, presents a copy to President Harry Truman. The RSV received wide acceptance, was the first translation to challenge the popularity of the King James Version, and launched a flood of Bible translations that has not stopped.

who used the principles of dynamic equivalence (see sidebar on page 89) to create an easily understood Bible. Although it is considered important because of its official status and scholarly translators, the NEB never really caught on.

NEW AMERICAN STANDARD BIBLE (NASB) (1963, 1971). In 1942, Dewey Lockman, a wealthy citrus farmer in Southern California, established a foundation to promote Christian evangelism, education, and benevolence. The Foundation's first Bible translation was the Amplified Bible, in which synonyms and definitions for many words are made part of the text. The NASB is a literal word-for-word translation that updates the ASV and is more conservative theologically than the RSV.

GOOD NEWS BIBLE (GNB) (originally called TODAY'S ENGLISH VERSION, TEV) (1966, 1976). Produced by the American Bible Society using the principles of dynamic equivalence, the TEV New Testament sold thirty million copies in the first five years and was endorsed by Billy Graham, the Roman Catholic Church, and numerous Protestant denominations. The GNB is written in simple, everyday language and is suitable to those for whom English is a second language, children, and those unfamiliar with the Bible. It was popular with Jesus People who were converted in the hippie culture of the 1960s and 1970s. In 1995 the American Bible Society published the CONTEMPORARY ENGLISH VERSION (CEV) as a substitute for the GNB.

THE LIVING BIBLE (LB) (1967, 1971). When Ken Taylor, who worked at Moody Bible Institute, tried to have devotions with his ten children, he found they did not understand the KJV or the RSV. But when he paraphrased a chapter he was reading, "they knew the answers to all the questions I asked!" Taylor formed Tyndale House Publishers to publish Living Letters, then Living Gospels, the New Testament, and in 1971 the complete Bible. Like any paraphrase, the Living Bible is interpretive, not a translation. It has been immensely popular, selling more than forty million copies. A translation made by a group of scholars using the principles of dynamic equivalence in the tradition of *The Living Bible* was published in 1996 as the NEW LIVING TRANSLATION (NLT).

NEW INTERNATIONAL VERSION (NIV) (1973, 1978). A group of evangelical Protestant Bible scholars funded by the sale of the headquarters build-

Chicago's Moody Bible Institute has been the most prominent school in America for providing an education in the Bible for pastors, missionaries, Christian education workers, and musicians. Founded in 1886 by evangelist Dwight Moody, the school also developed a publishing program, a radio network, and a training program for missionary pilots. The picture from 1892 shows faculty and students. In the center is the Institute's first president, R. A. Torrey. Today more than four thousand students study the Bible on Moody's main campus in downtown Chicago and on satellite campuses in Spokane, Washington, and Plymouth, Michigan.

When Ken Taylor asked his children questions after reading the Bible, they would just shrug their shoulders. But when he explained what he had read by paraphrasing the Bible, "they knew the answers," and those paraphrases led to his producing The Living Bible. *When Billy Graham offered it to his listeners, it became a bestseller, eventually selling more than forty million copies.*

ing of the New York Bible Society[161] made an entirely new translation with the goal that it be accurate, beautiful, clear, and dignified and suitable for public and private reading, teaching, preaching, memorizing, and liturgical use. The NIV has become, according to its publisher, Zondervan, the most popular modern English translation of the Bible. A revision, TODAY'S NEW INTERNATIONAL VERSION (TNIV), was published in 2002 and 2005.

THE NEW KING JAMES VERSION (NKJV) (1979, 1982), the latest of a number of revisions of the KJV, intended to retain the beauty and majesty of the KJV while updating some of the language. The work was commissioned by Thomas Nelson Publishers. However, unlike the RV, ASV, RSV, and most other modern translations, the New Testament is translated from a Greek text based on the Byzantine family of manuscripts similar to the Greek text the translators of the original KJV used.

THE MESSAGE: THE BIBLE IN CONTEMPORARY ENGLISH (1993, 2002) is a paraphrase by Eugene Peterson, a Presbyterian pastor. In the introduction Peterson says the goal of his paraphrase is "to convert the tone, the rhythm, the events, the ideas [of the Bible] into the way we actually think and speak."

ENGLISH STANDARD VERSION (ESV) (2001) is an evangelical revision of the RSV. It is more literal than the NIV, more conservative than the RSV, and easier to read than the NASB. The translators say it is "an essentially literal translation, emphasizing word-for-word precision" but at the same time retaining as much of the literary power of the KJV as possible.

Not only has there been a proliferation of Bible translations since the publication of the Revised Version in 1881, but Bibles are increasingly available in a variety of colors, bindings, and formats—a camouflage cover for outdoorsmen, a little princess Bible for girls, and a "Biblezine" for teenage boys, for instance. Bibles are also distinguished by the amount and type of added material—reference Bibles, family Bibles, and study Bibles. Influential study Bibles include the Scofield Reference Bible, the Open Bible, and the Ryrie Study Bible. And translations of the Bible are available in audio recordings, online, and in a variety of electronic formats.

And what more shall I say? For the time would fail me to tell of debates concerning science

In addition to a variety of translations, the Bible is available with a variety of features and in many formats. "Biblezines" are Bibles in magazine format with pictures and articles interspersed with the text of the Bible. Revolve *(pictured here) is for teenage girls;* Refuel *is for teenage boys;* Becoming *is for women;* Align *is for men; and* Bibleman Combat Manual *is for boys ages 6 to 10.*

161 The New York Bible Society became the International Bible Society and is now named Biblica.

162 Barna Research Online, "The Bible," www.barna.org. This information is based on 1993 figures, according to Michael J. Vlach, "Americans and the Bible: Bible Ownership, Reading, Study and Knowledge in the United States (www.theologicalstudies.citymax.com/page/page/1572910.htm [accessed August 27, 2009]).

163 Barna, 2006 figures.

and Scripture, controversies over Bible reading in schools, of the Bible's use in liberation theology, of the founding of Bible institutes, Bible conferences, Bible churches, and much more.

Between World War I and World War II the Bible began to lose influence in America. Churches became less focused on their beliefs and more focused on their social gatherings. Americans stopped using biblical terms in their conversations and began to talk in secular and nonreligious terms. The Bible was separated from the marketplace and the classroom as part of a campaign to separate church and state. America was no longer a nation filled with biblical images, biblical language, and biblical teaching.

But even so, 92 percent of American households have a Bible[162] and an astonishing 47 percent of Americans told researchers that they read the Bible at least once a week outside of church.[163] In spite of that, there is widespread ignorance about what the Bible says. For a multitude of Americans the Bible is still truth above all truth, but it is no longer the story above all stories. Many Americans say they believe the Bible, but too often they are not sure what it says.

BIBLE TRANSLATION THEORY

Do all the Bibles say the same thing? Usually, but not always. The last sentence in Romans 16:20 says, "The grace of our Lord Jesus Christ [be] with you. Amen!" (Young's Literal Translation); "I pray that our Lord Jesus will be kind to you" (CEV); "May the undeserved favor of our Lord Jesus be with you all." (Cotton Patch Version); or "Enjoy the best of Jesus!" (The Message).

A Bible translator has to choose between faithfulness to the original text and readability. When a literal translation runs into a problem, it just translates the words and lets the reader figure out what they mean. When a paraphrase runs into a problem, it interprets the original words for the reader. The problem comes when the interpretation does not accurately convey the meaning or nuances of the original.

Acts 10:44-45 tells of the Holy Spirit falling on all those who heard Peter preach. The NASB, a literal translation, says, "All the circumcised believers who came with Peter were amazed, because the gift of the Holy Spirit had been poured out on the Gentiles also." Circumcision was the physical evidence that a male was a good Jew and so "circumcised believers" is a way of saying "Jewish believers." "Circumcised believers" is what Luke wrote, but since American readers may not understand the cultural background, the NLT translates Acts 10:45, "The Jewish believers who came with Peter were amazed that the gift of the Holy Spirit had been poured out on the Gentiles, too." *The Message* takes its paraphrase one step further and also explains "Gentiles": "The believing Jews who had come with Peter couldn't believe it, couldn't believe that the gift of the Holy Spirit was poured out on 'outsider' non-Jews."

The two approaches to translation are called formal equivalence (meaning as close to a word-for-word translation of the original language as possible) and dynamic equivalence[164] (meaning a translation gives the equivalent of the original thoughts, even at the expense of literally translating all words or keeping the original word order). The NASB adheres to formal equivalence. At the other extreme, *The Message* makes very free use of dynamic equivalence. The NIV attempts to balance the two.

Where the question of whether all Bibles say the same thing gets interesting is with Bible translations that advocate a point of view. The King James Version followed Wycliffe and Tyndale by not translating the Greek word *baptizo*, but merely transliterating it as "baptize." Alexander Campbell's[165] revision of the King James New Testament in 1826 was one of a number of "immersion" translations that render *baptizo* as "immerse" instead of "baptize." The American Bible Society had a no-win debate over the issue with the result that the American and Foreign Bible Society was formed in 1836 to publish "immersion Bibles."

The New World Translation (1950,1961) was made by the Jehovah's Witnesses, and although it is a fairly literal translation, it has some peculiarities that reflect Jehovah's Witness teaching. For instance, Jehovah's Witnesses teach that Jesus was not God and so John 1:1 is translated, "In the beginning was the Word [referring to Jesus], and the Word was with God, and the Word was a god" instead of the "the Word was God" (KJV).

One translation principle of the RSV was that the Old Testament should be translated without taking into account New Testament interpretations. The most controversial result is Isaiah 7:14 where the KJV says, "Behold, a virgin shall conceive, and bear a son, and shall call his name Immanuel," which the RSV translates as, "a young woman shall conceive and bear a son."

The more strongly a translation follows the principles of dynamic equivalence—the more of a paraphrase it is—the more the point of view of the translator will appear. This is particularly true because paraphrases such as *The Living Bible* and *The Message* have tended to be done by individuals, whereas more literal translations such as the NASB or the NKJV have tended to be done by committees.

One other controversial practice in Bible translation is the use of gender-neutral language. The NIV, for instance, has published an edition that sometimes changes KJV's "man" and "brothers" to "human beings" and "brothers and sisters."

164 The term *dynamic equivalence* was coined by American Bible Society translator Eugene A. Nida.
165 The Churches of Christ and the Disciples of Christ trace their heritage to Alexander Campbell's teaching.

9

"TO THE END OF THE EARTH"

(Right, clockwise from top left): Lansdale, Pennsylvania; Yunnan Province, China; St. John the Evangelist *by Piero della Francesca; Tanzania; Middle East; Eastern Europe; Afghanistan; San Francisco; Ethiopia; Jerusalem; Chicago; Bushnell, Illinois; Ghana; Thailand; (in center, to right of Thailand): Los Angeles; (in center, below Thailand): Macks Creek, Missouri.*

"MY NAME IS MARY JONES, SIR. DO YOU HAVE ANY BIBLES FOR SALE?"

Mary Jones was a sixteen-year-old Welsh farm girl. Her father had died when she was four, and she and her mother had to work hard to survive. When Mary became a Christian at eight, her passion was to read the stories in the Bible for herself.

"Mary, we don't have money to buy a Bible," her mother said. But Mary was determined and sold eggs from chickens a neighbor had given her, washed people's clothes, and took care of children. For six years the young girl saved her pennies to have enough money to buy her very own Welsh Bible, but the nearest place to buy one was from Rev. Thomas Charles in Bala, more than twenty-five miles away.

"I know it's a long ways, but God will go with me," said Mary, and she walked barefoot so that her shoes would not wear out.

"I'm sorry, but I promised the last Bible I have to someone else a few days ago," Rev. Charles said. But seeing the tears in Mary's eyes and hearing her story, he decided that the other person could wait a little longer. He could not send Mary back home empty handed.

But that is not the end of the story. A short time later Rev. Charles was at a meeting of the Religious Tract Society in London and told Mary's story in a discussion of the tremendous need for Bibles. The Tract Society did not feel it could meet the demand and so a new organization was formed to supply Welsh Bibles. "And if for Wales, why not for the Kingdom? Why not for the whole world?" said one of the men at the meeting. The new organization was The British and Foreign Bible Society.

HOLY
BIBLE
79
87
19

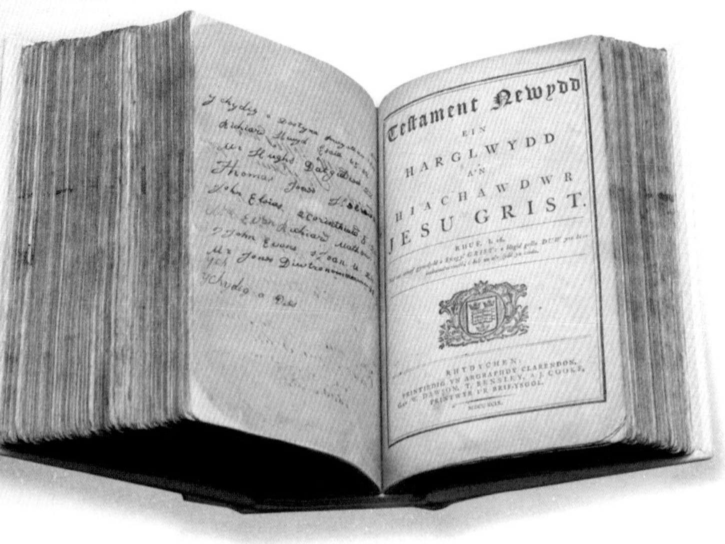

The sale in 1800 of this Bible by Rev. Thomas Charles to eight-year-old Mary Jones, who lived in what is now Gwynedd, North Wales, was the inspiration that led to the founding of The British and Foreign Bible Society. The translation of the Bible into Welsh was made by William Morgan in 1588 and revised in 1620. Like the King James Version in English, this Bible was the one book a family would own. It was instrumental in keeping Welsh a living language, inspired Welsh literature, and helped to maintain a Welsh national identity.

The Bible had been translated into Latin, German, English, and other languages wherever Christians went, and there have always been Christian missionaries—from the apostle Thomas going to India to Pope Gregory's sending Saint Augustine to Britain in the sixth century. In the nineteenth century missionary efforts exploded. Catholics did not promote Bible study, but Protestants did and translated portions of the Bible into nearly five hundred languages and dialects by 1900. Today at least one book of the Bible is translated into more than 2,400 of the world's 6,909[166] living languages. Each of these 2,400 translations has its own story, and three organizations—the Bible Societies, Wycliffe Bible Translators, and the Jesus Film Project—stand out in the effort to make the Bible available in the heart languages of people "to the end of the earth."[167]

A Bible Society is an organization formed for the purpose of translating, printing, and disseminating Scripture, traditionally without note or comment. The British and Foreign Bible Society was the first (1804) and has supplied Bibles to the whole world. It has published more than half a billion Bibles or portions in seven hundred languages. It was the first of 145 Bible Societies that now make up the United Bible Societies.

The movement quickly spread, and by 1816 one hundred independent Bible Societies were in the United States. In spite of Britain's being at war with the United States,[168] the British and Foreign Bible Society gave between $300 and $500 to each of the state societies. In 1816 the American Bible Society was formed.

The American Bible Society has conducted campaigns to give Bibles to every family in America and distributed the Bible to servicemen and women, to immigrants in their own languages, to seamen, and has placed Bibles in hotels—a task that was taken up in 1908 by the Gideons, an organization founded by three Christian traveling salesmen. The American Bible Society has also employed colporteurs who have traveled across the country, from farms to lumber camps to prisons, sometimes selling and sometimes giving away Bibles.

Like its British counterpart, the American Bible Society has published Bibles translated by missionaries throughout the world in more than one thousand languages. Eugene A. Nida, a linguist and former Executive Secretary for Translations, tells an interesting story of a missionary translating "God redeemed us" in Bambara, spoken in Mali, West Africa. The literal translation for the phrase in Bambara is "God took our heads out." The Africans had memories of Arab slave traders forcing men and women to walk in chains and with heavy iron collars

166 6,909 according to http://www.ethnologue.com/ (accessed August 27, 2009).
167 See Acts 1:8.
168 The War of 1812, which lasted until 1815.
169 Eugene A. Nida, *God's Word in Man's Language*, (New York: Harper & Row, 1952), 13-14.

around their neck. If a chief or king saw someone in the line he wanted to free, he would have to pay the slave trader for the person and then take his head out of the iron collar. Nida explains, "God saw us in slavery to sin and self, being driven under the lash of Satan, and so He sent His Son to die that men might live. He took our heads out."[169]

Requests from Africa and the Far East for a Bible for people who speak English as a second language led the American Bible Society to translate and publish *Today's English Version* (also called the *Good News Bible*) in 1966 (New Testament) and 1976 (Old Testament). Its popularity, especially of the paperback New Testament, was immense.

While most of the state Bible Societies have turned their work over to the American Bible Society, the New York Bible Society, founded in 1809, changed its name to the International Bible Society and moved to Colorado and later changed its name again to Biblica. It is the copyright holder of the New International Version, which, it says, is "the world's most widely read contemporary English translation of the Bible."

In 1987 the United Bible Societies and the Amity Printing Company in Nanjing, China, entered into a cooperative agreement to print Bibles and New Testaments in China. Since then, more than fifty million Bibles and nine million New Testaments have been printed there, with 85 percent of them being for distribution in China itself.

It was a hot, sunny Good Friday in 2008, when a group of women singing and dancing welcomed guests arriving on the small airstrip in Pindiu, Papua New Guinea. In the distance kundu drums played while dancers led a procession of men carrying seventy-four boxes of Kube New Testaments. For twenty years Yong-Seop Lee and his wife, Hyeon-Sook, had learned Kube and translated the New Testament. German missionaries had gone to the Pindiu area almost one hundred years earlier, but it was not until the Lees, who are Wycliffe Bible Translators, finished their work that the nearly ten thousand Kube people could read the New Testament in their own language. "Now God has moved inside the Kube," the school's headmaster said.

Bible Societies employed colporteurs to sell Bibles wherever they could, including marketplaces and door-to-door. Their work frequently included street preaching, praying with people, and giving Bibles at no cost to those who could not afford to pay. The American Bible Society used colporteurs in the United States and in China. This 1924 picture shows a New York Bible Society colporteur loading his car in New York City.

Since 1942 Wycliffe Bible Translators has translated Scripture into more than six hundred languages of people who did not have access to any portion of the Bible and in many cases that did not have any written language at all.

The organization traces its beginnings to 1917 when Cameron Townsend was sent to Guatemala to sell Bibles. At the time, missionaries to Central America would learn Spanish and then try to teach it to the Mayans so that the Indians could read a

Spanish Bible. When a Cakchiquel man said to Townsend, "If your God is so great, why can't he speak my language?" Cameron Townsend realized that if he translated the Bible, God could speak Cakchiquel. In retrospect, the world's best ideas seem simple. Just as Gutenberg's invention of movable type seems obvious today, Cameron Townsend's translating the Bible into Cakchiquel does not seem unusual. It just took thirteen years of determination, hardship, faith, and concern for the Cakchiquel people for the translation to become a reality. Townsend had to adapt the Spanish alphabet to Cakchiquel and develop a technique for teaching people to read.

When he learned that there were hundreds of people groups in the world without a written language and that fifty such groups were in Mexico, Townsend began a program called Summer Institute of Linguistics (SIL) to train Bible translators. He took students to Mexico to put into practice what they learned. Townsend next went to Peru and later "Uncle Cam" and his wife made eleven trips into Caucasia, which stretches from Turkey north into Russia.

More than forty thousand translators have been trained through SIL courses around the world. Today Wycliffe is in ninety-three countries translating the Bible into two thousand minority languages and enabling minority people to establish and control their own identities.[170]

In 1999 Wycliffe leaders realized that at their then current rate of starting one translation every eighteen days, it would take until 2150 to begin translation of the Bible into the nearly than twenty-four hundred languages that still needed the Word of God. Translation work was accelerated and in November 2008 a campaign was launched with the goal of having all translations in progress by 2025 so that everyone can hear the Word of God in his or her own heart language.

More than one million Bibles a month are printed in Nanjing, China, at the Amity Printing Company and sent throughout China through a network of more than seventy distribution points. Since 1987 Amity has legally printed more than sixty million Bibles and New Testaments in sixty languages and Braille.

ALTHOUGH THE WORDS OF THE BIBLE HAVE BEEN transmitted through ink on paper for more than twenty-five hundred years, it is the words that are important, not the form. The most watched film in history is not *Gone with the Wind*, not *Star Wars*, not *Titanic*, but the gospel of Luke, called simply *JESUS*, and known as "the *JESUS* film." The English version is derived primarily from the *Good News Bible*.

When Bill Bright, founder of Campus Crusade for Christ, met John Heyman, a producer and entertainment entrepreneur, they formed a partnership that ultimately led to the creation of the film of Luke, which was originally intended to be part of a motion picture of the entire Bible. Five hundred scholars made sure the film was historically accurate, and every day's

170 One fascinating project that grew out of the work of Cameron Townsend is The Ethnologue, a catalog of the world's languages, number of speakers, and locations. Originally published periodically in paper and ink, it is now available on the Internet at www.ethnologue.com.

171 According to The JESUS Film Project, the movie has been viewed more than six billion times, which includes repeat viewings. Comments that the figures were not scientifically gathered has led to the more vague but still incredibly impressive "several billion."

172 Franklin Foer, "The Passion's Precedent: The Most-Watched Film Ever?" *New York Times*, February 8, 2004.

173 Wendy Murray Zoba, "Bill Bright's Wonderful Plan for the World," *Christianity Today*, July 14, 1997, 24.

shooting in Israel was carefully reviewed. *JESUS* was a box office failure in 1979, and the rest of the Bible was never filmed. But in 1980 The JESUS Film Project, a division of Campus Crusade for Christ, began translating it into other languages. Now there are more than one thousand, including Karakalpak (Uzbekistan), Farsi (Iran), Shona (Zimbabwe), Dani (Indonesia), and Shipibo-Conibo (Peru). The film has been shown to several billion people[171]—nearly half the people in the world—and "has resulted in more than 225 million men, women and children indicating decisions to follow Jesus."

The *JESUS* film has been shown in New York City, and tapes and DVDs of the film have been distributed to every home in Hawaii, South Carolina,

TODAY AT LEAST ONE BOOK OF THE BIBLE is translated into more than 2,400 of the world's 6,900 living languages.

Alabama, and other states. But the focus has been on showing it to people who may have never seen a movie and never heard the Bible in their own language. More than five thousand missionaries have shown *JESUS* from high in the Andes to isolated Pacific islands to African townships and jungles.

When the film was shown to three hundred fifty people in a remote village of South Africa with no electricity, it was the first movie most of them had ever seen. "You could see them physically jump back at the sight of the serpent tempting Jesus," said the missionary, Brian Helstrom. "When soldiers whip Jesus, you could hear grown adults crying." When a missionary told the people they could become Christians, "One hundred forty-five people walked out of the darkness into light." [172]

When a missionary couple were on the way to a village in Peru to show the film, they were stopped by terrorists, who stole their projector and the film. Later one of the men sought out the couple to tell them because the terrorists were bored, they had watched the film seven times, and that he and others had become Christians. [173]

The *JESUS* film is the most widely circulated portion of the Bible in history.

The culmination of Charles and June Foster's more than fifty years of living with the Bakaonde people in northwestern Zambia was the publication of the Bible in 1975 in Kikaonde. Here Charles works with an assistant to translate the Bible so that the nearly 250,000 Bakaonde people will have, he said, "a clear view of God's great love and how He sent His Son that through His death, we have redemption."

Inhabitants of the small island of Wuvulu, north of Papua New Guinea, speak Wuvulu-Aua. This family looks through the New Testament, translated by James A. Hafford of Wycliffe Bible Translators, at the close of its dedication in July 2005.

LIKE MARY JONES, THE NEZ PERCES, A NATIVE American people living in what is now Idaho, longed to read the Bible. Someone—perhaps a fur trapper, perhaps a member of the Lewis and Clark expedition—had told them of a book that would teach people how to better serve their Creator. Six Nez Perces chiefs were sent east to find "the Book of Heaven." Two died along the way, and in 1831 four arrived in Saint Louis and were taken to meet the explorer General William Clark, who showed them the wonders of Saint Louis. While in the city, two of the four remaining chiefs died. Before going home to tell their people that they had not found the Book of Heaven, the two who were left were given a banquet in their honor by General Clark. One made this speech,

> My people sent me to get the white man's Book of Heaven. You took me where you allow your women to dance, as we do not ours, and the Book was not there. You took me where they worship the Great Spirit with candles, and the Book was not there. You showed me images of the good spirits and pictures of the good land beyond, but the Book was not among them to tell us the way. I am going back the long, sad trail to my people of the dark land. You make my feet heavy with gifts, and my moccasins will grow old in carrying them, yet the Book is not among them. When I tell my poor blind people, after one more snow in the big council, that I did not bring the Book, no word will be spoken by our old men or our young braves. One by one they will rise up and go out in silence.
>
> My people will die in darkness, and they will go on the long path to the other hunting grounds. No white man will go with them, and no white man's Book, to make the way plain. I have no more words. [174]

The Nez Perce chiefs walked nearly two thousand miles home and had to wait almost fifteen years. The first printing press in Idaho printed portions of "the Book of Heaven" in Nez Perce in the 1840s.

Today nearly twenty-four hundred people groups are still waiting for the Book of Heaven.

THE *JESUS* FILM

The most watched film in history is the gospel of Luke, called *JESUS* and known as "the *JESUS* film." You can watch all two hours of the film in French Spanish, Bhujpuri, Ge, Icelandic, or more than one thousand other languages—including English—by going to http://www.jesusfilm.org/film-and-media/watch-the-film. Just choose the language you want to see.

174 Athur T. Pierson, ed., *The Missionary Review of the World* (New York: Funk & Wagnalls Co., September, 1902), 642-43. This speech was originally reported in the *Christian Advocate and Journal*, March 1, 1833.